ADVANCE PRAISE FOR *FINDING BLISS*

GENERAL COUNSEL

"This is an important book for all of us interested in the future of our great legal profession. Too many lawyers are unhappy in outdated models. *Finding Bliss*—with its wonderfully challenging title—discusses the many innovative ways the profession is changing and how to change it much, much more. For better, more flexible and happier careers and happier clients as well."

Brackett B. Denniston III, Senior Vice President
& General Counsel, General Electric Company

"I was personally inspired to improve our focus on flexibility by Debbie's first book *Law & Reorder*, so I looked forward to reading this new collaborative book *Finding Bliss*. I've read a lot about innovation, diversity and flexibility, or lack thereof, in law, but this book puts them together in a new way that I hope will have a significant impact on our profession. I've spent years complaining about the slow pace of change in the legal profession, especially with respect to diversity. After reading Finding Bliss, I'm more optimistic about our prospects for innovation and inclusion looking forward."

Michelle Banks, Executive Vice President Global Responsibility
& General Counsel, Gap Inc.

"Debbie once again demonstrates that she is at the forefront of anticipating changes in the market for legal services. Her insights in *Finding Bliss: Innovative Legal Models for Happy Clients & Happy Lawyers* provide an important template for those trying to innovate the way in which lawyers deliver value and support to their clients."

Denise F. Keane, Executive Vice President
& General Counsel, Altria Group, Inc.

"Leveraging technology, creating career paths, improving spending predictability, building a more inclusive profession—this book tackles all of the strategic issues on my administrative agenda. At a time in which our profession needs innovation for sustainability, this resource is an insightful thought-starter on all of our most important issues."

Colleen Batcheler, Executive Vice President, General Counsel
& Corporate Secretary, ConAgra Foods

"*Finding Bliss* offers a compelling overview of the state of the legal profession today, unpacking old traditions like the corner office and billable hours, and showing us rather the variety of legal practice models. In describing the motivations, challenges and pressure points of lawyers in all different modes of practice, whether in firms or in house or anywhere in between, *Finding Bliss* charts where the profession may be headed tomorrow. Enlightening reading, especially for the general counsel."

Rachel R. Stern, Senior Vice President,
Strategic Resources and General Counsel, FactSet

"We are seeing only the beginning of the revolution in the delivery of legal services in the US. *Finding Bliss* provides real insight and helpful guidance for those truly interested in servicing their clients' in a new era."

Amy Fliegelman Olli, Senior Vice President
and General Counsel, Avaya

"We all have heard that General Counsel are under relentless pressure to manage and control their legal spend. And, as experienced corporate achievers, we will figure out some way to accomplish this. But most of us do not wish to do so in a way that is unduly damaging to law firms. We are, after all, lawyers. And many of us came from the very firms that we now have to 'manage and control.' *Finding Bliss* is a welcome guide to creating what some think impossible: a model where happy lawyers—both in-house and in firms, happy law firms, and happy corporate clients all coexist. Focusing on seven levers that General Counsel can operate (innovation, value, predictability and trust, flexibility, talent development, diversity and inclusion, and relationship building) to increase happiness while managing and controlling costs, the authors provide a wealth of practical suggestions. *Finding Bliss* is a thoughtful and useful addition to the toolkit of all lawyers who are interested in changing the legal profession for the better."

Suzanne Day, Vice President & General Counsel,
The Lubrizol Corporation

"This excellent book describes the changing demands of the legal marketplace, explains the forces driving these changes and offers experience-based, practical advice on how lawyers across the spectrum of settings can succeed. In *Finding Bliss*, Debbie Epstein Henry and her co-authors remind us that the challenges of today's law practice provide ample opportunity for the rewards of practicing law. In *Finding Bliss*, Debbie and her co-authors pull no punches in describing the challenges of practicing law today. The message of the book, however, is decidedly positive. The demands of the marketplace, which are pushing the evolution of how legal services are delivered, are creating great opportunities that match up well with the skills and desires of many talented lawyers who have found the traditional legal service delivery model less than satisfying."

Keith A. Smith, Executive Vice President
& General Counsel, Carolinas HealthCare System

LAW FIRM MANAGING PARTNER

"There is no question that market forces are bringing tremendous change to the profession. Much has been written about the various challenges, but never has anyone attempted to bring it all together by addressing in one volume not only the challenges, but proven strategies to turn challenge into opportunity. Comprehensive without being superficial, *Finding Bliss* fills that gap by bringing the reader a variety of proven methods and means to align client, law firm, and lawyer interests. Every law firm leader and general counsel will find something in these pages to improve their organization."

Wally Martinez, Managing Partner, Hunton & Williams, LLP; Former General Counsel, Diageo North America, Inc.

CONSULTANTS & INNOVATORS

"I read this book with an eye toward whether it would be of value to my clients. Clearly it is important in its messaging and equally important in its recommendations. As law firms struggle to maintain profitability they will need to be more innovative in terms of service delivery and staffing models. This book gives invaluable advice and recommendations on how to do so. I will be putting it on my recommended reading list for law firm leaders and managers."

Tom Clay, Principal, Altman Weil, Inc.

"Law as a field is undergoing a rolling transformation as it adopts to the parallel forces of globalization and technology that have transformed other fields. But lawyers as individuals are often struggling, as their training and experience has not fully prepared them to embrace this 'New Normal.' Debbie Epstein Henry lays out a realistic, lawyer-friendly roadmap for lawyers to understand the changes around them, embrace the new pieces that make sense for them, and preserve the best of their professional values and aspirations. I don't know too many blissed-out lawyers, but reading *Finding Bliss* will certainly help any lawyer up their bliss quotient."

Paul Lippe, CEO, Legal OnRamp

"Lawyers are under no professional obligation to be miserable, even though the ranks of dissatisfied and unfulfilled attorneys nationwide seem to tell a different story. Fortunately, however, outdated business models that relentlessly pressure lawyers to work, bill and conform are finally giving way to flexible, sensible and accessible legal enterprises that replace 'square-peg' thinking with unique assessments of lawyers' real value. Deborah Epstein Henry expertly describes this new landscape, analyzes its enormous potential for reshaping the legal market, and delivers an engaging guide to a happier and more highly valued legal profession."

Jordan Furlong, Principal, Edge International; Publisher, Law21

WOMEN THOUGHT LEADERS

"Once again Debbie Epstein Henry is forging a new and critical path for the legal profession. *Finding Bliss*, it turns out, is not an oxymoron for the legal profession. With a keen eye on the necessity for (and inevitability of) innovation, flexibility, diversity and talent development, the authors paint a new and appealing reality emerging for lawyers and their clients. *Finding Bliss* is a must-read, offering a path back to meaning and purpose for lawyers, and a reasonable bottom-line for all."

Claire Shipman, Senior National Correspondent, Good Morning America; Author, Womenomics *and* The Confidence Code

"*Finding Bliss* is the ultimate guidebook for how legal industry reform can be achieved at both the institutional and individual levels. The book expertly shows the reader how to seek and align the goals of increased profitability and productivity—as well as true satisfaction—for clients, lawyers and legal employers. The interspersed teachings from legal luminaries bring depth and perspective to a profession desperately in need of the invaluable wisdom that *Finding Bliss* brings. This one is not to miss!"

Carol Evans, President, Working Mother Media; Author,
This is How We Do It: The Working Mothers' Manifesto

"In *Finding Bliss*, Debbie, Suzie and Garry do not just talk about the concept of 'happiness' in the abstract or as an emotional state—they provide a unique and comprehensive roadmap for creating a sustainable business model within a law firm or corporate legal department that promotes productivity and economic success. This thoughtful and thought-provoking treatise is a must-read for all of those seeking to improve the legal profession."

Lisa M. Passante, President,
National Association of Women Lawyers

"Every young lawyer and law student interested in knowing their options, taking control of their career, and understanding how the legal market is changing needs to read *Finding Bliss*. Debbie, Suzie, and Gary offer concrete tips, examples of successful but varied career paths, and new options for lawyers who want to define their own career path. *Finding Bliss* recognizes that there is no single 'right' path in the legal profession and provides an important counter-narrative to the one that law students and young lawyers typically hear. In short, you cannot afford not to read it."

Katherine M. Larkin-Wong, President, Ms. JD

ACADEMIC REPRESENTATIVES

"*Finding Bliss* offers an insightful analysis of the challenges facing the legal profession today. By counseling both a need to innovate and a return to core values, such as sound ethics and meaningful relationships, it offers an innovative new paradigm to enable attorneys and clients to fulfill their goals in a mutually empowering way."

Gillian Lester, Dean, Columbia Law School

"Early in my career at Yale, I taught a popular course called Psychology and Law. Missing from the classroom, however, was much about the actual psychology of lawyering. And I knew nothing about innovative new models for the legal profession that could produce far more satisfied clients and especially fulfilled legal professionals. Debbie Epstein Henry and her co-authors have filled that void with *Finding Bliss*. I am not surprised; in her previous book, the award-winning *Law & Reorder*, Debbie taught us how to achieve a balance between work and family life in a legal career. Now, she and her co-authors have written a clear and compelling guidebook to the future of lawyering. Partners and associates at firms large and small, traditional and cutting-edge, will learn much from this beautifully written volume, and so will their teachers."

Peter Salovey, President and Chris Argyris Professor, Yale University

"*Finding Bliss* reminds us that the 'new normal' is anything but. The legal profession is undergoing significant restructuring, and with these changes will come both challenges and opportunities for lawyers, clients and law firms. This book offers concrete advice on how to find professional growth and satisfaction by refusing to remain bound by tradition and instead remaining flexible and open to emerging alternatives."

Rachel F. Moran, Dean & Michael J. Connell Distinguished Professor of Law, UCLA School of Law

"*Finding Bliss* is a nonfiction page turner that will make you put down your John Mortimer, Scott Turow, and John Grisham. Its authors prove that the death of law is exaggerated while presenting seven concepts that can lead to meaningful, successful and satisfying legal work. It's a crisp, readable, insightful and persuasive must read for providers and consumers of legal services, and certainly for any educator responsible for preparing students for the new world of law."

Nicholas W. Allard, President and Dean,
and Joseph Crea Professor of Law, Brooklyn Law School

"*Finding Bliss* will open your eyes to how the legal profession is changing and how the changes will affect law firms, in-house legal departments, law schools and lawyers. Law school administrators, law professors and law students—indeed, anyone who wants to understand the legal marketplace and how to best position law students for future success—will benefit from this book."

Bruce Green, Stein Professor of Law & Director at Fordham Law
School, Louis Stein Center for Law and Ethics

FINDING BLISS

BLISS

**Innovative
Legal Models for
Happy Clients &
Happy Lawyers**

DEBORAH EPSTEIN HENRY
SUZIE SCANLON RABINOWITZ
GARRY A. BERGER

FINDING
BLISS

Innovative
Legal Models for
Happy Clients &
Happy Lawyers

Foreword by **ANNE-MARIE SLAUGHTER**

Cover design by Kelly Book/ABA Publishing.

Printed in the United States of America.

18 17 16 15 14 5 4 3 2 1

ISBN: 978-1-62722-652-3
e-ISBN: 978-1-62722-653-0

Library of Congress Cataloging-in-Publication Data
Henry, Deborah Epstein, 1967– author.
  Finding bliss : innovative legal models for happy clients & happy lawyers / Deborah Epstein Henry, Suzie Scanlon Rabinowitz, Garry A. Berger.
    pages cm
  Includes bibliographical references and index.
  ISBN 978-1-62722-652-3 (alk. paper)
  1. Lawyers—Job satisfaction—United States. 2. Practice of law—United States—Psychological aspects. 3. Law firms—United States. 4. Legal services—United States. I. Rabinowitz, Suzie Scanlon, author. II. Berger, Garry A., author. III. Title.
  KF300.H457 2015
  340.068'8—dc23
2014041387

Discounts are available for books ordered in bulk. Special consideration is given to state bars, CLE programs, and other bar-related organizations. Inquire at Book Publishing, ABA Publishing, American Bar Association, 321 N. Clark Street, Chicago, Illinois 60654-7598.

www.ShopABA.org

DEDICATION

To our parents: Sylvia and Stanley Epstein, Karen and Dan Davis, and Joan and David Berger.

For your love and inspiration to value family—both in our homes and in our work.

DONATION

We are grateful for the contributions that these non-profit organizations have made in our lives and in the lives of so many others. In an effort to help extend their impact and to raise greater awareness of their efforts, we have chosen to donate to each of them a portion of the proceeds of this book.

- LaGuardia Community College Foundation,
  https://www.laguardia.edu/Supporters-Friends/
  Mission-Statement

- American Bar Association Commission on
  Women in the Profession,
  http://www.americanbar.org/groups/women.html

- Autism Speaks,
  http://www.autismspeaks.org

CONTENTS

3

Predictability and Trust

James W. Cuminale, Chief Legal Officer, Nielsen N.V.

4

Flexibility

Jean Molino, General Counsel, McKinsey

ABOUT THE AUTHORS

Deborah Epstein Henry

Deborah Epstein Henry is Co-Founder and Managing Director of Bliss Lawyers, a firm that provides high caliber temporary part-time and full-time lawyers in "secondments" where the lawyers work at in-house legal departments and law firms yet they are employed by Bliss. The firm is a new legal model that oper-ates administratively from a virtual platform, with employees in a dozen states and counting.

Debbie is also an internationally recognized expert, consultant and public speaker on the future of the legal profession, new legal models, women's issues and work/life balance. She is the author of *LAW & REORDER*, the #1 best-selling American Bar Association Flagship book for 2011. A former practicing litigator, Debbie is President of Flex-Time Lawyers LLC, a consulting firm she founded in the late 1990s, providing consulting, training and speaking services to law firms, companies and non-profits in the U.S., Canada and Europe. Her firm is well known for running Best Law Firms for Women with *Working Mother* magazine—a national survey to select the top 50 law firms for women and report on industry trends. Debbie's expertise with respect to women and workplace issues spans a range of subjects including retention, promotion, networking and business development, sponsorship, women's initiatives, workplace culture and structure, leadership, compensation, self-promotion, flexibility, re-entry, and work/life balance. Through her public speaking and consulting, Debbie has grown her network of lawyers to over 10,000 and through this network, she has done recruiting for more than a decade.

Debbie has garnered visibility for her work from *The New York Times*, NBC Nightly News with Brian Williams, *The Wall Street Journal*, National Public Radio, *The National Law Journal*, among many others. She has received numerous awards, including most recently, the 2012 *Philadelphia Business Journal "Women of Distinction"*. Debbie is a member of the Forum of Executive Women and she donates her time to a number of non-profits, including the Task Force for Talent Innovation, the American Bar Association Commission on Women in the Profession and Pace University School of Law's New Directions program. She received her B.A. in Psychology from Yale and her J.D. *cum laude* from Brooklyn Law School. Debbie clerked for the Honorable Jacob Mishler in the United States District Court for the Eastern District of New York. She is married and the mother of three sons, ages 19, 16 and 13.

Suzie Scanlon Rabinowitz

Suzie Scanlon Rabinowitz is Co-Founder and Managing Director of Bliss Lawyers. Suzie recently launched SRD Legal Group which is a women owned virtual law firm as an alternative for companies of all sizes committed to working with women and minority owned law firms. Suzie has been a partner at the virtual law firm of Berger Legal LLC for more than ten years and prior to joining the virtual law firm world, she worked as a traditional lawyer at the law firms Sullivan & Cromwell and Wachtell, Lipton, Rosen & Katz. Suzie also worked at the National Association of Securities Dealers (predecessor to FINRA) and in the New York State Executive Chamber of Governor Mario M. Cuomo as a Press Aide. She earned her law degree from Fordham Law School, where she served as the Annual Survey Editor of the *Fordham Law Review* and was the recipient of the American Jurisprudence Award for Torts and Criminal Law. She received her B.A. in medieval studies from Sarah Lawrence College with honors. Suzie is a recent graduate of the Goldman Sachs 10,000 Small Businesses program which is a scholarship based entrepreneurship program for business owners.

Suzie is the founding board chairperson of the Danbury Hospital Associate Board and currently serves as a Director of the LaGuardia Community College Foundation. She has also served as Board President of Maimonides Academy of Western Connecticut, Vice President of the Board of Directors of The Ridgefield Playhouse, Executive Vice President of the Board of Trustees of Temple Shearith Israel and Co-Chair of the Windward School Annual Fund. She is married and the mother of two sons ages, 16 and 14.

Garry A. Berger

Garry A. Berger is Co-Founder and Managing Director of Bliss Lawyers. Garry is a pioneer in the legal services industry, having founded Berger Legal LLC in 2002, an innovative virtual law firm which has grown to include some 15 senior attorneys serving Fortune 500 clients as well as small to mid-size companies

across a variety of industries. He previously worked as an in-house lawyer at The Thomson Corporation (now Thomson Reuters) in Stamford, Connecticut. Garry spent three years at Weil, Gotshal & Manges in New York City and two years as a judicial law clerk to a federal judge in the Southern District of New York. He earned his law degree from Columbia University School of Law, where he was a Harlan Fiske Stone scholar and Research & Writing Editor of the *Columbia Journal of Law and Social Problems*. Garry received his B.A., *magna cum laude*, in politics, from Brandeis University. He is a founder and serves on the Danbury Hospital Associate Board and founded and leads Ridgefield Little League's Holland Division for special needs children. Garry is the father of two sons, ages 15 and 13.

ACKNOWLEDGMENTS

In writing this book and running Bliss Lawyers, we could never have done it without the support of our families. While many authors thank their families on the home front, which we will do, of course, we also want to thank our families on the work front. We say that because our business has actually been built as a modern family business, our Modern Family, if you will.

Bliss Lawyers is the union of our three families, spanning the country from New York to Connecticut and Pennsylvania to California. Our first colleagues included each of our siblings as well as Suzie's husband. Many companies emphasize their belief in family values. We actually live and breathe that belief—both operationally and in how we treat our clients and lawyers. So we want to start by thanking, as well as introducing, our family and Bliss Lawyers' colleagues, whose names are listed in the photograph below, along with ours, in the order in which they appear.

Dan Rabinowitz, Jeff Berger, Garry Berger, Debbie Epstein Henry, Suzie Scanlon Rabinowitz, Elissa Davis, Joel Epstein, Shannon Horn

We are so grateful to our family members not only for their hard work and diligence in keeping Bliss Lawyers running while we were steeped in writing this book but also for their love and sense of humor that make our work not only stimulating and exciting but also simply fun. As our business has grown, we are thankful to have new colleagues who have become invaluable contributors to our extended family, including Shannon Horn and Renee Newell. Shannon's meticulous proofreading and fact checking and Renee's precise attention to detail were instrumental in fine tuning this book and ensuring a high quality end product.

Words cannot express our gratitude to Goldman Sachs 10,000 Small Businesses and LaGuardia Community College for giving us the idea to write this book. The guidance we received from Rod Dauphin, Assuanta Howard, Javis Brunson, Demica Durr, Paisley Demby and Louisa Johnson was invaluable. Thank you for showing us—the lawyers in the program—how to identify opportunity instead of always only seeing risk. We continue to reap the benefits from the lessons we learned along with the wonderful relationships and connections that we developed. We would be remiss not to also acknowledge Jane Schulman, who is a driving force behind 10,000 Small Businesses, for elevating the entire teaching profession with her enthusiasm and commitment to small businesses. We at Bliss Lawyers will always be thankful for being selected as one of Goldman Sachs' 10,000 Small Businesses.

We are delighted to have the American Bar Association publish our book. The guidance, creativity, attention and excitement generated by Tim Brandhorst is unparalleled. We know that the unwavering support as well as the inspirational ideas developed by Sonali Oberg will be instrumental to the book's promotion as will be the public relations' initiatives of Neal Cox and the social media outreach of Laura Vecchia. The detail-oriented focus of the ABA's copyright team was also critical to the professionalism of this project.

Our editor, Stuart Horwitz of Book Architecture, was an invaluable partner in writing this book and we are grateful to Vernā Myers for the generous introduction. It was not just Stuart's enormous gift as an editor and a critical thinker that brought this book to another level. Stuart's expert guidance in book structure, tone, flow and wit elevated our ideas and content to a final manuscript for which we are truly proud. We attribute our ability to keep motivated and stay on track to Stuart's steadfast enthusiasm, flexibility and top notch organizational skills. We also owe a debt of gratitude to our beta readers, Patricia Gillette and Samuel Silver, whose candor and legal profession insights brought our ideas into sharper focus and tested our theories with constructive scrutiny that enabled us to continually revise and improve.

We are humbled by Anne-Marie Slaughter's generosity in writing the insightful Foreword to our book. We could not have asked for a more fitting person to set the context for our discussion, given Anne-Marie's like-minded vision of the need for change on both the institutional and individual levels. We are deeply grateful for the precious time she took to endorse our work and her willingness to use her platform to enhance our profile.

We are honored by the inspirational writings provided by our eight thought leaders who each introduced one of the chapters of our book. These include: William D. Henderson, Professor of Law and Val Nolan Fellow, Indiana University Maurer School of Law; Randal Milch, Executive Vice President and General Counsel, Verizon; James W. Cuminale, Chief Legal Officer, Nielsen N.V.; Jean Molino, General Counsel, McKinsey; Daniel B. Rodriguez, Dean and Harold Washington Professor, Northwestern University School of Law; Thomas L. Sager, Partner, Ballard Spahr LLP; Michele Coleman Mayes, Vice President, General Counsel and Secretary, The New York Public Library; and Gretchen Rubin, Author, *The Happiness Project* and *Happier at Home*. We are privileged to include the wisdom of each of these luminaries on the issues that we agree are critical to improve the delivery of legal services. With their initiative and our aligned interests, we know that our objectives in this book will be more readily achieved and implemented in law firms, in-house legal departments and beyond.

We are also deeply grateful to our clients and colleagues who have provided insights that we have woven throughout the chapters of this book. They have been so helpful to us and we appreciate the opportunity to now share their teachings to a larger audience who we know will benefit from their wealth of knowledge and experience. We are also thankful for our Bliss Lawyers' employees who work for our Fortune 500 companies and law firm clients across the country. Facilitating our employees' ability to work and thrive in a new legal model and a different way of practice has brought true gratification for us in our work and in our lives. Both our clients and our lawyers inspire us every day to live by our motto of "Happy Clients, Happy Lawyers."

Debbie also wants to take this opportunity to thank her family. My husband, Gordon Henry, has been my partner in love and in life and in raising our three sons. He is the one who has enabled me to squirrel away in my office or get on that flight for a presentation or meeting when the needs arise. Gordon has also served as my constant advisor and confidant in all of the critical decision making in our lives. I am eternally grateful for Gordon's love and willingness to be there for me so that together, we can meet the ever-increasing demands at home and work. My parents, Sylvia and Stanley Epstein, are the anchors in my life. They have given me the foundation and inspiration to live a fulfilling life of love, family, humor and engaging work. I am grateful to Susie Rubin for her clever copywriter phraseology as well as the never-ending wisdom she provides as my older sister. Don't worry Susie—it's only a matter of time before you join our brother Joel's ranks as a member of the Bliss team! To Joel, I am grateful for the opportunity we have to work together, bringing our already close relationship to another level of love, trust and strength. I also want to acknowledge my mother-in-law, Sondra Henry, who has been unyielding in her support, enthusiasm and interest in my work and in our lives. My sons, Oliver (19), Spencer (16), and Theodore (13) are the ones who truly inspire and amaze me. They gave me both the motivation and the confidence to start my own businesses, giving me more control and flexibility to be there for all of the important—and not so important—things in their lives. I'm nostalgic for their younger years but equally excited to watch them continue to grow into the bright, kind, energetic contributors they will be to others and to the world. What I wish for them is the ability to find love, friendship, satisfaction, passion, humor and success both at home and at work.

Suzie would also like to thank her family for their love, support and encouragement. My husband, Dan Rabinowitz, has been my partner in raising my boys for the past five years and has allowed me to achieve a level of professional success that I never thought imaginable. Dan is not only the Chief Financial Officer of Bliss, but CFO of our household. He manages both roles with a sense of humor, kindness, skill and commitment that is unparalleled. I am also grateful to my sister Elissa Davis who helps us with the talent management component of the business and so much more. Working closely with my sister for more than eight years has allowed us to have a greater presence in our children's lives because we are able to step into each other's shoes professionally and always be available for our children when we are needed. I am eternally grateful to my parents, Karen and Dan Davis, for telling me I could accomplish anything and for showing me firsthand the importance of hard work, helping others and family values. I would also like to thank my wonderful mothers-in-law Carol Mackay and Judy Rabinowitz for being so supportive of my career and always thinking I am terrific even when I fall short. You make me feel like I am six feet tall! My precious and precocious boys, Max (16) and Brice (14), have motivated me to set an example of hard work in our home. I hope each of you can find a path that brings you happiness and satisfaction.

Garry would like to say thank you to his parents, Joan and David, who owned and operated a "Mom and Pop" pharmacy for some 30 years. You surely inspired the entrepreneurial spirit I've always had within me. You set the bar in terms of how to successfully run a business—it is something I often think about and have tried to emulate in my own businesses. I would also like to thank my two amazing boys, Max (15) and Harry (13). After graduating law school, I began with a "tried and true" career track—clerkship, New York City law firm, in-house job—I loved these first jobs in the legal profession. I learned about the practice of law from different vantage points and, just as importantly, made many friendships along the way which I continue to cherish today. But becoming a father to Max and Harry served as my inspiration to leave the expected career path and establish something new and different. My decision to found a virtual law firm in 2002 was due largely to my desire to spend more time with my boys. I have been fortunate over these many years to be able to work from home, doing interesting work for my clients and working with an amazingly talented group of lawyers—all while being home for the school bus each day, driving to afternoon activities and being "hands on" in raising my children. I often say that I believe I have spent more time with my kids during their years growing up than most dads get to spend in a lifetime, and this is not something I take for granted.

My work at Berger Legal led to my decision to join with my dear friends, partners and sisters in life, Suzie and Debbie, to create Bliss Lawyers. I am so fortunate to work with such talented, smart, passionate, caring and hard-working women, and I love them both dearly. Bliss Lawyers also brought me together with my brother Jeff, who is one of the key players in our organization. Working with Jeff has been the icing on the cake that is Bliss Lawyers. I am looking forward to many more years working with my Bliss family. I hope that through our work at Bliss Lawyers and by writing this book we are both opening up career possibilities for others and generating some creative thinking in our field. One of the mantras I try to live by is "Go All In," and I like to think I have done that so far in my career. I wish the same for my colleagues in the profession. I also say things like "Invest in Shoes," "Call Your Mom" and "Just Kiss Her"—I am not sure they are applicable here, but these are nonetheless such valuable words of advice that I would be remiss if I did not share them.

There are many others who we have all met along the way for whom we are also thankful. If we neglected to name you personally, our apologies. We are truly grateful for all who have made this journey possible.

FOREWORD

ANNE-MARIE SLAUGHTER

Bliss and law are two words that the vast majority of the public, and certainly the vast majority of lawyers and law students, are likely to think of as an oxymoron. And yet, over my 12 years as a law professor, I often found my bliss teaching, thinking, and writing about law. I would open my civil procedure classes by saying, "Law is the etiquette of ritualized battle." I would then explain to my students that law is the substitute for violence in resolving human disputes, and thus is the backbone of peaceful order. From my vantage point as an international relations scholar who must focus regularly on the chaos, insecurity, and danger posed by failed states, a system of "ritualized battle" is an extraordinary and indispensable achievement for human flourishing.

But law is so much more. It is about battle but also about victory—the victory of right rather than might. In resolving a dispute, a judge must interpret text in light of words and ordinary meaning.

When those guides are not enough, as they often are not, she must choose the interpretation that best reflects both good policy and deep underlying social, political, and economic values. Law absorbs and reflects our highest aspirations for human society and self-government, an ever-evolving effort to capture and define our desires as lawmakers in ways that will stop lawbreakers. It is also a set of tools for problem solving, allowing a good lawyer not simply to tell a client what she may and may not do but also to figure out how to help her do what she wants to do within the law.

I would also tell my students the famous anecdote involving Justice Oliver Wendell Holmes and Judge Learned Hand, another of the country's greatest jurists. Watching Holmes drive away in his carriage after lunching together, Judge Hand is reported to have run after him, crying, "Do justice, Sir, do justice!" Holmes purportedly stopped his carriage and said, "Justice? What's that? That is not my job. My job is to apply the law."

Holmes notwithstanding, justice is one of the deepest and most elemental human emotions, as any parent can tell you. "That's not fair" is a sentiment that children feel from almost the minute they can talk. Law does not always achieve justice by any means, but it is the principal human instrument by which we as a society strive for it.

These are lofty sentiments. They often animate the hearts of students deciding to go to law school, and guide the aspirations of a law school's graduates. I did my best to inculcate them in my own students, while assuring them that they could use law as a foundation for whatever they wanted to do in life. At the same time, as the years passed, I knew that the majority of my students would not be happy as lawyers.

The partners of big New York firms who interviewed me as a second-year student in the fall of 1983 saw themselves as members of a learned profession, generalists relied on by their clients for their wisdom and judgment as much as for their knowledge of a specific case or problem. They were men (and they were indeed almost entirely men) who knew and respected their colleagues as genuine partners in a collective enterprise. And to hear them tell it, they lived rich and satisfying lives, with time for public service, hobbies, reading, and, for those men who made it a priority, family. My students were heading into a very different world, one in which BigLaw had become big business, elevating the cult of billable hours into a culture of time macho, substituting the quantity of input for the quality of output.

Women were the first to get off the bus. The conventional narrative about women and the law is that, as in business, women enter law firms in equal numbers and with the same potential as their male peers, but then fall off the career ladder as their cohorts ascend toward the higher rungs. According to the statistics in Chapter 6, although women have comprised between 40 and 50 percent of law school graduates for decades, they still account for no more than 17 percent of equity partners in law firms.

In my article "Why Women Still Can't Have It All," published in *The Atlantic* in June 2012, I attributed their disappearance to the inability of large law firms to create flexible enough structures and working conditions to keep them. It was thus no surprise to me that one of the first efforts to think about how law could really be practiced differently came from Debbie Epstein Henry. I quoted her first book, *Law & Reorder*, in the article and have discussed its findings with many audiences of women since.

In reading the pages of this book, however, I see a different picture. It is becoming increasingly clear to me that in law, as in other industries, women are not apart but merely ahead. They are the canaries in the goldmine, signaling that the air is becoming increasingly unbreathable *for everybody*. They leave big firm practice not simply because firm rigidity over schedules and career paths makes it impossible for them to fit their caregiving and breadwinning responsibilities together successfully, but also because their work no longer provides the mix of money and meaning, profits and purpose that makes law worth practicing in the first place.

Consider Suzie Scanlon Rabinowitz's story. As related in Chapter 4, she worked for two top New York law firms after graduating from law school. In the late 1990s, however, law firms became unsustainable for Suzie once she understood that the expectations were inconsistent with her lifestyle, so she left the profession. The flexible nature of Garry Berger's virtual law firm environment is what brought her back to practice. But as all three authors of this text affirm eloquently, "the focus needs to be on why and how incorporating more flexibility into every workplace is in the best interests collectively of clients, law firms, and lawyers. Indeed, flexibility is not just the future of work—it is its present as well."

The fragility and flaws of the current large firm model of law practice becomes all the more evident in the harsh light of global competition. When I left law teaching in 2002, over a decade ago, that competition was manifesting itself primarily through the challenge posed to big New York firms by big London firms, institutions such as Linklaters and Clifford Chance that had long had a practice as global as the British Empire. Today, global competition takes place on many different disaggregated dimensions of legal practice, as the authors detail in Chapter 1. Just as U.S. radiologists are discovering that films can be read and interpreted more cheaply and just as easily by medical technologists in India, litigators are finding that document management can be outsourced more cheaply and effectively than they can do it themselves.

But competition breeds innovation. The question asked and answered in many rich and fascinating ways in this book is what kind of innovation? The higher, harder, faster approach to practicing law simply is not working and will never be America's competitive advantage. Lawyers and law firms must return to the parts of law that sustain hearts as well as minds: the sense of actually helping a client to accomplish a worthy goal; the importance of exercising judgment, a quality that cannot simply be reserved for judges; the excitement of solving important problems that align private gain with public good; the satisfaction of marrying knowledge, experience, and creativity in ways that provide a path through an apparently impenetrable thicket of difficulties.

Finding Bliss describes many different types of innovation that offer lawyers a much more satisfying career path that can offer flexibility, a wider range of assignments that deliver on law's traditional promise of allowing generalists to flourish, and the disaggregation of different levels and types of legal work to provide many more jobs for non-lawyers. It tackles the roots of many problems currently plaguing the legal field, from the lack of trust not only between lawyers and clients but also among lawyer colleagues to the issue of how to measure the value of individual lawyers, their work, and firms as a whole.

"Happy Clients, Happy Lawyers." That is the motto of Bliss Lawyers. It seems an impossible dream. But law, properly understood, is not only an area of human endeavor that is central to the ability of humans to flourish individually and together but also a helping and caring profession. Representing those who cannot speak for themselves, resolving disputes that tear people apart and block productive enterprise, making deals that help people advance their businesses and their dreams are all functions that can engage the mind and satisfy the heart, offering meaning and purpose at different levels of society.

What is needed is a way of doing this work that does not turn all of life into hours to be billed, an endless sucking maw of client obligations. The legal profession needs to reinvent itself, as a source of work and a way of life. *Finding Bliss* provides a guide.

INTRODUCTION

It is not the strongest of the species that survives, nor the most intelligent; it is the one that is most adaptable to change.
—Charles Darwin[1]

We know you might be skeptical, picking up a book called *Finding Bliss*, especially given the tumult in the legal profession since 2008. In fact, you may be wondering if the authors of this book are clueless. Well, we want to assure you that—no—we are not naïve. We know things have been bleak, and we are well aware of the portended demise of legal services. We have read the same predictions as you about the shrinking need for lawyers. But even with all of this, we believe that there are real opportunities to be had in the legal profession of the future. And, if you are strategic and creative and willing to take some calculated risks, you will be among those who benefit from them.

Each of the co-authors of this book have decades of experience in the legal profession. We all started our careers conventionally— in federal clerkships and New York City large law firm associate

---

1. This quotation was originally paraphrased by Leon C. Megginson, Professor of Management and Marketing at Louisiana State University at Baton Rouge from Charles Darwin's *Origin of Species*. Along the way, Megginson's paraphrase was slightly changed and turned into an actual quotation from *Origin*. University of Cambridge, "One Thing Darwin Didn't Say: The Source for the Misquotation." *Darwin Correspondence Project*, last modified 2014, http://www.darwinproject.ac.uk/one-thing-darwin-didnt-say.

roles. Ultimately, we chose less traditional paths. This book is the story of our lessons learned and our views on how to thrive—not just survive—in today's volatile and changing legal market. We share this knowledge based on our own research and investigation, as well as from our first-hand experience.

In this book, most often, you will hear from a collective voice about the changes in the legal profession and the means to more effectively deliver legal services that better align the skills of the talent pool with the needs of the client. However, each of us has had independent experiences and developed select expertise. Where a view is derived from one of us individually, we single out that voice.

The distinct paths of the three co-authors led to the formation of Bliss Lawyers, a new legal model that hires high-caliber lawyers to work on "secondments" (temporary engagements) in corporate in-house legal departments, as well as law firms. These secondments, at times, lead to the seconded (borrowed) lawyer converting into a permanent employee of the company or law firm. In running this successful new legal model for nearly four years, we have gained insights and a vision about the legal profession that we believe will bring value to share with law students, lawyers, clients, law firms, and other legal service providers[2].

DEBORAH EPSTEIN HENRY

Deborah (Debbie) Epstein Henry's journey to Bliss began in 1999, when she was practicing as a commercial litigator and struggling to figure out how to both play an integral role in her kids' lives and be on partnership track. She sent out an e-mail to three colleagues and three other lawyers who were similarly situated—lawyers who wanted to be active parents as well as successful professionals—to start a brown bag lunch group for support and networking.

---

2.   Our use of the term "legal service providers" throughout the book is meant to broadly encompass law firms and other companies and firms that provide services in the legal profession to clients including those that practice and do not practice law.

Within a few days, 150 lawyers e-mailed her back in response. As Debbie continued to be flooded with e-mails, she knew she had struck a nerve.

After three years of running pro bono events on work-life balance and women's issues at large law firms, Debbie decided to convert her growing expertise and launched a consulting practice in 2002. She stopped practicing law and began a New York chapter of what became known as Flex-Time Lawyers LLC. Her consulting practice emerged from advising legal employers and lawyers about work/life balance and other issues impeding women's retention and promotion, such as business development and networking, sponsorship, workplace culture and structure, leadership, compensation, self-promotion, flexibility, and re-entry.

In 2009, Debbie started researching and writing her first book, *Law & Reorder: Legal Industry Solutions for Restructure, Retention, Promotion & Work/Life Balance* (American Bar Association, 2010). Prior to this, she had been focused mostly on women and the individual action steps they could take to improve their status in the profession. Writing *Law & Reorder*, Debbie recognized that the significant challenges facing women and others in the legal profession were only half the problem. The other half was the legal model—i.e., the existing infrastructure of law firms and in-house legal departments. Thus, with the release of *Law & Reorder*, Debbie's focus expanded. She sought to discover not only what lawyers could do to improve their status but also how legal employment models could be redesigned to better meet client needs and enable everyone in the talent pool to thrive in a profitable business structure.

GARRY A. BERGER

Garry A. Berger did not know exactly what it meant to be a lawyer. He had the academic credentials, graduating *magna cum laude* from Brandeis University and receiving the designation of Harlan Fiske Stone Scholar at Columbia Law School. After law school graduation, Garry landed a prestigious federal clerkship. While he knew he would begin his career in a large law firm, he also knew he did not see a future for himself there. He did not want to live in or commute to New York City, and he had no desire to make partner at a traditional firm. Perhaps because he grew up in a family of entrepreneurs (his parents owned a pharmacy for 30 years where Garry got his first job), he was destined to be more independent.

After working for several years each as an associate at Weil, Gotshal & Manges LLP and as in-house counsel for The Thomson Corporation (now known as Thomson Reuters), Garry founded his own law firm, Berger Legal LLC, in 2002. His desire to innovate had additional impetuses beyond being raised with entrepreneurship. His son had just been diagnosed with autism, and Garry was looking for more flexibility—he knew the ability to be at home would make a big difference for him in overseeing the care of a special needs child. His previous experience had shown him that one of his strengths was dealing with internal business clients, and the idea of running a virtual law firm crystallized in his mind.

Like Debbie, Garry found that a lot of women, in particular those who worked in large law firms, needed more and different opportunities. Many wanted to work virtually with flexible hours and could do so while producing an excellent work product. For the first six years of running Berger Legal, Garry felt the stigma against a law practice being operated virtually. He did not take pains to advertise that he was working from his attic. Around the time of the economic downturn, however, all of that changed—the fact that his virtual team of lawyers allowed him to charge less to his Fortune 500 clients for the same or better quality work became a distinct selling point.

SUZANNE SCANLON RABINOWITZ

Suzie began her career working for two different large New York City law firms after graduating Fordham Law School at the top of her class—a fact that she attributes to requiring less sleep in her youth than any other law student in New York City. She quickly realized, however, that the traditional law firm was not her ideal career path when she was warehoused in a conference room in San Francisco, looking for negative covenants in investment advisor agreements for days on end.

Wanting to start a family, Suzie exited the practice of law entirely for five years. Once Suzie's children attended pre-school, however, she again found herself needing intellectual stimulation and adult engagement. So she volunteered for everything she thought worthwhile from the parent–teacher organization in her children's school to founding an associate board at Danbury Hospital in Connecticut, and serving on The Ridgefield Playhouse Board of Directors.

Through Suzie's extensive volunteer work and leadership in her kids' school, she met Garry who had a son attending the same school. When Suzie learned about the virtual firm Garry had recently launched and his need for lawyers to work on a flexible basis, she decided to join him, handling corporate transactional work and intellectual property agreements—the deal-making, non-confrontational aspects of lawyering that she enjoyed the most.

As the needs of Berger Legal clients shifted, so did Suzie's work; one client asked her to come work in-house on a sensitive project. This made her, in essence, Berger Legal's first seconded lawyer. This experience helped Suzie understand the importance of relationship building with her clients and the value of developing creative solutions to manage legal workflows. It also ultimately showed Suzie the true value of secondments first hand. All the while, Suzie remained active in her kids' lives and in the volunteer work of her community—not only a silver lining of the virtual law firm job but also a flexibility and lifestyle requirement.

FINDING BLISS

The founding of Bliss Lawyers brought Debbie, Garry, and Suzie together into a dynamic partnership, made official in 2011 but with its roots in 2008.

While Debbie was promoting her first book, *Law & Reorder*, which was released in late 2010, she held events in 13 major markets, with prominent panels of household name general counsel, top law school deans, and managing partners from leading law firms. What struck her was that every high-profile general counsel participant, regardless of industry or geography, said the same thing: They were getting pressure to reduce their outside counsel budget and do more work internally—yet they were not getting authorization to increase headcount. They had much less certainty about their staffing needs and, in turn, their companies were seeking greater staffing flexibility by engaging highly skilled lawyers for temporary assignments. Rather than always hiring an outside law firm, these general counsel were increasingly turning to secondment firms—at about one-third to one-half of the price of a conventional law firm—to perform some of the traditional law firm work. These general counsel also expressed a frustration about having to absorb the real estate costs of their outside law firms, knowing that part of the basis for these law firms' high rates was their overhead.

As Debbie's visibility grew through her international consulting, writing, and press attention, Flex-Time Lawyers grew from those first 150 e-mail contacts to a network that today boasts over 10,000 lawyers across the country. Beginning in 2003, Debbie naturally became a recruiting go-to for legal employers and lawyers. In 2008, Debbie and Garry reconnected, 15 years after they were summer associates together at Weil, Gotshal. Berger Legal's impressive roster of corporate clients kept asking to borrow the firm's lawyers, and they no longer had enough lawyers to lend from the virtual law firm. Yet Garry did not want to disappoint his clients for fear that they would go elsewhere.

Garry and Suzie turned to Debbie, knowing she had amassed a vast network of well-credentialed lawyers who were seeking an alternative to the 2,400 billable-hours track. Thus, beginning in 2008, the three began to fill secondments together through Berger Legal. In 2011, when the demand became so great, Debbie, Garry, and Suzie decided to merge their networks of lawyers and clients to create a secondment firm that gave both clients and attorneys a new way of working together.

Deliberately, they chose not to house their internal operations in a bricks and mortar office. Instead, they elected to build the business infrastructure virtually, leveraging the virtual platform that was a significant factor in growing Berger Legal. This was a means to provide more competitive pricing to clients while being able to still provide generous compensation and benefits packages to lawyers. The goal was to be the first thriving business founded on merging two innovations—the secondment and the virtual firm.

The other goal was to make diversity a signature of their work, and they were able to achieve this by founding a majority women-owned, operated, and controlled business certified by the Women's Business Enterprise National Council (WBENC). The diversity focus was an obvious one for Debbie, given her longstanding role as an advocate for lawyers including re-entry moms and those with less linear career paths, as well as people of color and lawyers seeking more flexibility. These concerns meshed seamlessly with the socially responsible roles that Suzie and Garry have played in their community and through Berger Legal. A fresh view of the legal talent pool was key to the innovation of this new legal model. Thus was born Bliss Lawyers, a readily accessible bench of A-list talent ready to work for Fortune 500 companies and law firms across industry sectors in a dozen states and counting.

WHAT WE HAVE LEARNED AND WHAT WE WANT TO SHARE

Our backgrounds are important context for understanding the messages we hope to impart in this book. Our collective experiences have taught us how traditional and new model firms can more effectively deliver legal services and how to align the skills of today's and tomorrow's lawyers to better meet clients' needs. Finding new and successful ways for clients and lawyers to work together is the principal focus of this book. Because we believe that success in the legal profession hinges on the alignment of the employment model and individual talent, each major concept in this book is examined through two lenses: the institutional and the individual. Indeed, we believe future success in the legal profession will require change at both the institutional and individual levels, as the two are inextricably linked.

Traditional and new model firms can more effectively deliver legal services by focusing on seven key concepts: Innovation; Value; Predictability and Trust; Flexibility; Talent Development; Diversity and Inclusion; and Relationship Building. These seven concepts are the means to maximize the talent pool's performance and delivery of legal services. Hence, these are the seven substantive chapters of this book that represent our observations of what needs to be improved, on both an institutional and individual level, as follows:

1. *Innovation.* In today's volatile market, facilitating innovation must be everyone's focus. It is not just about creating new legal models but also about the innovations created from within traditional models by both individual lawyers and employers.

2. *Value.* When we talk about value, we mean three things: how to value a representation for a client; how legal service providers can otherwise provide more value to a client; and how to create multiple valued career paths for lawyers.

3. *Predictability and Trust.* Clients desire more predictability in the fees they can expect, and individual lawyers want more predictability and control in managing their work. All of this is built on trust, not only in the law firm–client relationship but within law firms and in-house legal teams as well.

4. *Flexibility.* Clients need more flexibility in staffing, and individual lawyers need more flexibility in the way in which they work to produce their maximum quality of work—and to enhance their life. Achieving these goals is critical, along with ensuring that business needs are met and colleagues and clients are not negatively impacted by individual needs.

5. *Talent Development.* The salient question is how to most effectively develop and support legal talent during the trajectory of a career—from law student to junior associate to seasoned lawyer to retiring counsel. The answer will hinge on all legal industry stakeholders assuming the time, cost, and responsibility of talent development.

6. *Diversity and Inclusion.* Designing a diverse and inclusive work environment will require an understanding of the contribution of diverse talent as well as the value of diverse choice in legal service providers. Finding new and more effective ways to combat unconscious bias will be instrumental in achieving these goals.

7. *Relationship Building.* Lawyers who are more effective at building a network and community are both more satisfied

and more effective in delivering legal services. While the needs of law firm lawyers and clients may vary with respect to relationship building, both need a foundation of support and collegiality to maximize their impact and success.

At the start of each chapter, we include introductions from thought leaders who we call luminaries. They include general counsel, a law firm partner, a law school dean, a law professor and an expert outside of law. The point of these introductions is to establish context and tone by having these visionaries provide their wisdom to frame the conversation. Interspersed in the book, we also include findings from other individuals—mostly in-house lawyers—who have taught us important lessons about how to be more responsive to client needs and the demands of the market.

CONCLUSION

In this book, we present the new reality facing law students, lawyers, clients, law schools, and law firms today. While we understand that there are a lot of challenges and legitimate anxieties facing those in the legal profession, our outlook is still positive. Our goal in *Finding Bliss* is to inspire readers like you to break out of traditional roles and thinking. We encourage you to be bold and creative to help ensure both your professional and personal success, and in turn, your happiness.

1

INNOVATION

WILLIAM D. HENDERSON, PROFESSOR OF LAW AND VAL NOLAN FELLOW, INDIANA UNIVERSITY MAURER SCHOOL OF LAW; PRINCIPAL, LAWYER METRICS, LLC

Bill Gates once said, "People often overestimate what will happen in the next two years and underestimate what will happen in ten."[1] That adage likely applies to law.

The following Innovation chapter catalogues a wide array of changes occurring in the market for legal services. The biggest change is that the traditional law firm model is no longer following its predictable pattern of growth. The fundamental tension is that law is an indispensable input to a highly interconnected, digitized, globalized, and regulated world. Yet, we are now at a point where each unit of economic growth probably produces two or three units of legal complexity. This is putting tremendous strain on the traditional law firm model to become more like the rest of the economy.

Continued

---

1. Bill Gates, Nathan Myhrvold, and Peter Rinearson, afterward to *The Road Ahead: Completely Revised and Up-to-Date* (New York: Penguin Books, 1996): 316.

WILLIAM D. HENDERSON, PROFESSOR OF LAW AND VAL NOLAN FELLOW, INDIANA UNIVERSITY MAURER SCHOOL OF LAW; PRINCIPAL, LAWYER METRICS, LLC *CONTINUED*

Specifically, over any period of time, cost goes down while quality and speed of delivery go up. This is the productivity imperative— and it now applies to law.

What we are witnessing now is a period of experimentation where both traditional providers and legal entrepreneurs are searching for creative, sustainable ways to do more for less. Some of these innovations are clever, yet there may be no way to prevent competitors from copying and even improving upon these new models. Other innovations may not be sustainable over the long haul because their current cost and quality advantages will slowly dissipate over time (e.g., cheaper labor or real estate costs, or better technology). Yet, through a process of trial and error, it will be these very risk takers who produce truly ingenious and sustainable models that will drive the legal industry in the decades to come. Several of them are mentioned in the pages below, albeit their most important innovations may be yet to come.

INTRODUCTION

We live in an era where sweeping and innovative changes are not just on the horizon for the legal profession; they are already in our midst. The need for new legal models as well as for large law firms to innovate has become increasingly pressing. A 2013 report conducted by The Center for the Study of the Legal Profession at Georgetown found that firms were driven to change by a combination of factors that include slow demand, overcapacity that leads to losses in productivity, client dissatisfaction with fee increases, dropping realization rates, and modest increases in profits per partner.[2]

Another significant pressure point for change is the trend of globalization, i.e., the global expansion of U.S. and international law firms. In response to declining economics, some large firms are making strategic assessments that a greater global footprint will be required to serve the needs of international clients. The firms pursuing global expansion are focusing more on Asia, Latin America and the Middle East, where they see opportunities for economic growth to be greater than in North America and Europe.[3] As some large firms move towards globalization, they will be increasingly impacted by the range of laws that govern law firm formation in different regions. A good example of this is the Legal Services Act of 2007 in the U.K. which allows new types of legal businesses called "alternative business structures," which permit non-lawyers to own and run legal businesses and become partners in law firms. The Act also permits external investment into legal businesses.[4] In the U.S., these issues are being critically analyzed by the American Bar Association's 20/20 Commission,[5] among others, and if the influence of the Act extends, it will no doubt trigger another series of innovations.

In the meantime, there are other compelling drivers that are making legal service providers think differently about their work and how it is being parsed out. Futurist Richard Susskind talks about another influencer—the growing work trend called disaggregation

---

2. The Center for the Study of the Legal Profession at the Georgetown University Law Center and Thomson Reuters Peer Monitor, 2013 "Report on the State of the Legal Market" (2013): 7, http://www.law.georgetown.edu/continuing-legal-education/executive-education/upload/2013-report.pdf.
3. Ibid. at 8.
4. Bar Standards Board, "Changes to Regulation: Legal Services Act," https://www.barstandardsboard.org.uk/regulatory-requirements/changes-to-regulation/legal-services-act/.
5. Jamie S. Gorelick and Michael Traynor, "For Comment: Discussion Paper on Alternative Law Practice Structures: American Bar Association Commission on Ethics 20/20," 2011, http://www.americanbar.org/content/dam/aba/administrative/ethics_2020/20111202-ethics2020-discussion_draft-alps.authcheckdam.pdf.

whereby work is becoming unbundled. Disaggregation makes work more readily separated to be performed in discrete tasks or aspects of a project.[6] Clients are more sophisticated than ever: They are unwilling to pay the same high prices for all legal work, and they can more easily insist upon this because of the disaggregation trend in work and the resultant variety in legal service providers that abound. Additionally, there is a shrinking circle of global elite firms doing "bespoke" (i.e., highly specialized) or critical "bet the company" work (where, perhaps, the very existence of the company is on the line, or at a minimum a significant matter is at stake).[7] This is the one type of work that is not price sensitive and increasingly, fewer firms have access to perform that work.

Many of the large law firms that exist below the bespoke tier are suffering, having lost some of their "bread and butter" work to new legal service providers and feeling the need to account much more closely for how they are billing and how they are delivering value. Where once the large law firms represented their clients from the start of a representation to its finish, they now find that much of the work has been dispersed to specialized service providers who can not only do the work more cost effectively but also with greater proficiency, as it is their exclusive or among their select areas of focus. In some cases, these alternate legal vendors are doing the work formerly done by associates because the client has balked at the price or has learned to resist junior lawyers being trained on their dime. As a result, these firms have been forced to become leaner and shrink their costs in order to survive. Matters have also become staffed differently—where once there might have been three associates for every one partner in a leveraged model, this traditional large law firm staffing model can no longer be sustained.

Some of the regional and mid-size law firms have taken away large law firms' business as well, as the economic downturn has

---

6. Richard Susskind, *The End of Lawyers?: Rethinking the Nature of Legal Services* (New York: Oxford University Press, 2010).
7. Ibid.

prompted clients to give up their attachment to being represented by name brand firms in less high profile matters in exchange for being able to take advantage of more competitive pricing. Additionally, traditional law firms have been disadvantaged in having to compete with new model firms, some of which are actually not law firms and therefore not bound by the same ethical rules and constraints that govern law firm practice. Clients are also keeping more work in-house, and when they do share the work, they need more predictability in their legal fees and more certainty in their budgets. They also want law firms to share in their risk in the representations by, for example, taking lower fees upfront and having an upside or bonus in the event of a demonstrated success. And finally, part of the driving force for large law firms to innovate are their own gross receipts and the lack of growth in their revenues per lawyer, as will be more fully explored below.[8]

Cost and improved efficiency are behind much of the legal market shifts. Work that can be commoditized and systematized is outsourced when possible, often to offshore enterprises allowing for a substantial savings to the client. Other sorts of legal provider innovations have been undertaken by large law firm "refugees" who grew tired of hearing complaints from their clients that their rates were too high and too unpredictable. Truly, innovation in the delivery of legal services is in full swing—that is not the question. Rather, the question is, where is all of this trending?

Below we will explore cutting-edge changes to the legal profession by examining six models that together comprise the innovation taking place in the legal field today: Process, Foundation and Information Firms; Virtual Law Firms; Secondment Firms; A Combined Virtual and Secondment Firm; Nontraditional Law Firms; and Evolved Traditional Law Firms.

---

8. Rachel M. Zahorsky and William D. Henderson, "Who's Eating Law Firms' Lunch?" *ABA Journal*, October 1, 2013, http://www.abajournal.com/magazine/article/whos_eating_law_firms_lunch.

PROCESS, FOUNDATION AND INFORMATION FIRMS

The *American Lawyer* reported in its 2013 revenue of the top 100 U.S. firms that these firms' revenue totaled more than $77 billion.[9] However, since the beginning of the recession, per-lawyer earnings for these large firms have remained stagnant.[10] In contrast, some new legal service providers report that they are tripling their revenue annually and, in some cases, these firms report that 80 percent of the work that they do was formerly done by traditional law firms.[11] What follows are some groupings of different types of newer legal service providers that we are calling Process, Foundation, and Information Firms. We believe these firms are part of what is behind the flattening of large law firm revenue. Note that some companies provide services in all or a combination of these innovative groupings.

Discovery and Document Review Firms

Discovery and document review firms typically manage and analyze documents for large litigations. The founder of one of these firms, Novus Law, estimates that document review, management, and analysis is a $40–$50 billion business.[12] Given their technology and resources, these firms are expanding or planning to expand into drafting briefs and motions, compliance, contract management and other areas as well.[13] Clients are drawn to these discovery firms because they believe that the more volume of this type of work that a company does, the better at the process they become; they certainly become more cost effective. One Novus Law client

---

9.   Aric Press, Am Law, "100 Analysis: The Super Rich Get Richer," The *American Lawyer*, April 28, 2014, http://www.americanlawyer.com/id=1202651706887.
10.   Rachel M. Zahorsky and William D. Henderson, "Who's Eating Law Firms' Lunch?" *ABA Journal*, October 1 2013, http://www.abajournal.com/magazine/article/whos_eating_law_firms_lunch.
11.   Ibid.
12.   Ibid.
13.   Ibid.

estimated saving 15–30 percent on individual cases that could have cost upwards of $3 million.[14]

Legal Process Outsourcing Firms

Legal Process Outsourcing (LPO) typically occurs when work is sent offshore to a lower cost jurisdiction such as India, China, Israel, or the Philippines. This is work that associates at large law firms used to do, yet many clients have realized that this work often does not require the services of a U.S.-based lawyer. The type of work performed by LPO firms typically includes: document review, litigation preparation, deposition summaries, legal research and writing, patent prosecution, contract management, compliance services and drafting of memoranda, trial and appellate-level pleadings and briefs.[15] As with discovery and document review firms, the benefits are largely increased economy and efficiency. There have been concerns about quality, security, confidentiality and ethics and, as a result, some companies have pulled back from the use of LPO firms. Other companies have turned to U.S.-based LPOs that, at times, have become more trusted.

Legal Support Vendors

Another significant area of growth is the different types of legal support vendors. The companies that fit this category are those appearing at annual LegalTech trade shows. Their commercial activity today amounts to $20–30 billion.[16] Some of these firms offer legal services, others offer legal products like software, and some provide both. Examples of firms that fall within this category are firms that handle e-discovery, compliance, and information

---

14. Ibid.
15. Deborah Epstein Henry, *Law & Reorder: Legal Industry Solutions for Restructure, Retention, Promotion & Work/Life Balance* (Chicago: American Bar Association, 2010): 28.
16. Rachel M. Zahorsky and William D. Henderson, "Who's Eating Law Firms' Lunch?" *ABA Journal*, October 1, 2013, http://www.abajournal.com/magazine/article/whos_eating_law_firms_lunch.

management. The common denominator in these firms is that technology has enabled them to bring more efficiency, cost-effectiveness, and scale to handling legal representations.

Legal Form Firms

The firms that fall into the legal form category range from what we are calling Do-It-Yourself Lawyering firms to those that provide sophisticated Web-based tools to lay out the deal-making and litigation processes and improve efficiency. One example of the latter is Practical Law, a Thomson Reuters company, which provides subscription-based online resources and support including practice notes, standard documents and clauses, checklists, toolkits, legal updates and state-specific guidance to its clients who are typically solo, small and large law firms as well as corporate law departments.

When we refer to Do-it-Yourself Lawyering firms, we include such companies as LegalZoom, CorpNet, My Corporation, Find-LegalForms, and My Pocket Attorney. Each of these enterprises is an example of the pressing need for lawyers to improve their own internal efficiencies as well as for legal services to be delivered more simply and cost-effectively directly to the consumer. These online resources are mostly in the areas of business formation and development, trusts and estates, and personal and family law, but it is likely that these subject areas will grow. In each case, the online resources serve basically as facilitating agents that enable lawyers and non-lawyers to fill out standard forms and agreements. Lawyers can thus bring more efficiency to their work, and non-lawyers can function without the expense of a lawyer. These resources cut into the economics of legal markets just the same as many of the other innovations discussed here. Do-It-Yourself Lawyering also brings to mind eLawyering, where a client can access a portal and interact online with his or her lawyer. For example, Rocket Lawyer is creating access to legal services online by offering legal documents and information that attorneys can obtain through a low monthly membership fee. This model enables the client to have potentially greater engagement and involvement and provides the benefit of a lawyer to guide the client through the process.

Access to Information Firms

Another category of innovative firms are those that provide access to information that was previously provided on a costly basis. One example is Legal OnRamp, which is an online system for Massive Online Legal Analysis (MOLA), enabling large teams of lawyers to tackle mega-projects and jumpstart legal department transformation. Another example is Fastcase, an online service that replaces the individual editors at Westlaw and Lexis who indexed individual cases with computer algorithms, allowing for quicker research. Fastcase advertises that it is the only legal research system that sorts the best results to the top of the list in the same way that Google does for general searches enabling lawyers to find the most important cases right away, no matter how many search results are generated.

Simmons & Simmons LLP is a UK firm that has explored innovation on a number of fronts. In terms of access to information, it developed a subscription-based online service called Navigator that offers standardized regulatory information across more than 85 jurisdictions, providing clients with information that might otherwise be very costly to obtain from multiple sources around the world. In her own practice, Suzie has observed that the Navigator service is often used to mitigate risk in connection with the cross-border distribution of marketing materials and securities. Many financial services firms recognize that mitigating risk while reducing the cost of regulatory legal fees is an acceptable practice of efficiently managing compliance obligations. Relying upon a subscription-based service also serves as an enhancement by expediting the turnaround of work product to keep up with the fast pace expected of in-house legal departments.

The above five groupings capture the current general trends in Process, Foundation and Information Firms. However, these companies are constantly evolving and pushing the boundaries in the types of work they can pursue. New companies are also regularly cropping up, and they will continue to use technology and creativity to bring more efficiency and cost-effectiveness to the delivery of legal services.

VIRTUAL LAW FIRMS

Among small- and medium-size law firms, traditional law practices are growing or remaining relatively stable, especially in smaller markets. That said, smart law firm leaders are always trying to anticipate where they can cut costs and the fact cannot be overlooked that the largest overhead expense for any traditional law firm is real estate. And, increasingly, the client is becoming aware that it is the one paying for a firm's space, and often the accompanying artwork on its walls. By taking away, or significantly reducing, the largest cost to a law firm, the game-changing innovation of the virtual law firm allows for a significant reduction in overall overhead. In turn, this becomes a sizeable opportunity for the virtual firm to charge its clients more competitive rates, thereby transferring part of its savings to its clients.

In the traditional law firm model, we have come to think of it roughly this way: One-third of law firm costs go to pay associate salaries, one-third supports partner salaries, and one-third covers the overhead.[17] The innovation of the virtual firm has been to significantly reduce nearly all of the one-third cost dedicated to overhead. We say "nearly one-third" because certain overhead costs, such as employee benefits and insurance, remain fixed. Yet the savings garnered still enable virtual firms to present a considerable price advantage to competitor firms.

So how does the virtual law firm model work? To capitalize on cost reduction, lawyers typically work from home—in fact, it is

---

17.   Deborah Epstein Henry, *Law & Reorder: Legal Industry Solutions for Restructure, Retention, Promotion & Work/Life Balance* (Chicago: American Bar Association, 2010): 21.

often individuals drawn to this kind of autonomy and flexibility who desire to work in such firms in the first place. Some of these individuals are large law firm partners who were able to generate client work, yet their clients could no longer afford their fees. These former law firm partners delight in the ability to retain their client base but charge more reasonable rates (from one-third to one half of what large law firms charge).

These virtual law firm converts are also drawn to the model because of the potential earning capacity. Lawyers who are principally responsible for generating the clients (i.e., "rainmakers") may keep up to 85 percent of what they bill, in contrast to the traditional law firm model where lawyers keep typically about 33 percent of their billings.[18] In addition to autonomy and flexibility then, there is the added lure of potentially increased earnings, while fees and rates are actually lower than what clients are used to paying—a very attractive package.

Working virtually is not without its challenges, of course. One is that a lawyer's or law firm's brand is not as easy to demonstrate without the conventional structure and office space. Some virtual firms have addressed the brand challenge by relying more heavily on pedigree in their selection of lawyers. For example, when the largest virtual firm, VLP Law Group LLP, began, its founder hired lawyers with top credentials from elite academic institutions and law firms as a way to demonstrate its credibility to prospective clients.[19] This has changed over the years since virtual law firms have gained traction, but the issue of prestige still remains. How do you build a brand with no office space and when part of your business development strategy is not to waste money on marketing dollars? In running Berger Legal for over a decade, Garry believes that ultimately, the brand a virtual firm builds is based on reputation and relationships. Once the firm is able to establish a reputation for

---

18. Ibid.
19. Ibid. at 23.

delivering high quality work at a reasonable fee, the referrals that follow through the relationships built are what transcend the bricks and mortar building that had once served as a proxy for prestige.

Another challenge is how to maintain a sense of collegiality when lawyers appear to be connected merely through a common e-mail signature line. Suzie feels that the collegiality at Berger Legal flows from its family-first culture. The team has an understanding that if an individual lawyer has a family or other emergency, someone else will step into his or her shoes and cover any outstanding work. While it is true that a lawyer who works virtually has to initiate human contact—it does not naturally occur around the water cooler—some of the typical "water cooler" problems do not occur either, such as wasting time or engaging in office politics. Contact with both colleagues and clients in a virtual setting must be more intentional because of the planning required. Interactions like phone calls, meetings, firm outings and events are likely to be more productive because the colleagues are more consciously engaged. Additionally, for lawyers who work at virtual firms, in-person meetings, use of technology including teleconferencing, Skype and FaceTime, as well as participation in community business and legal organizations all help virtual firms to establish a greater professional identity and presence.

Another virtual law firm challenge is the lack of definitive boundaries between work and home. Suzie's work, for example, is ever-present and is woven into everything she does; when she is having dinner with her family, she sees her office within view and it is a constant reminder of her pending matters. As a result, her children grew up in a home where their mother worked in an office next to the kitchen—she was available at important times, but was not necessarily available more often than if she worked outside the home. Navigating a mom who worked virtually, and observing her headset conversations, had an amusing side effect; instead of asking for a play date with their friends, her children would come in to her office with a proposal: "Mom, I'd like to make a meeting with Cole and Samantha. . . ."

SECONDMENT FIRMS

The notion of the secondment, as it applies to the legal profession, has been around for a while, as clients have regularly asked traditional law firms to borrow a high-caliber lawyer for a limited term. At times, it was to fill in for a parental or medical leave or to help with some other staffing transition. At other times, the secondment would fill the role of support for extensive work overflow or a gap in expertise that a client might identify. In such cases, the term "secondee" typically was used to describe a well-credentialed, borrowed lawyer staffed on selective work on an engagement basis in a corporate in-house legal department.

While the secondment model developed with traditional law firms filling these in-house gaps, the demonstrated need, and the legal service providers who have responded to that need, has expanded. The disaggregation of work, where it can more readily be separated out into discrete tasks, allows for independent secondment firms, not just law firms, to lend out lawyers to support in-house legal departments with their work overflow and other temporary work needs. These secondment firms are not handling "bet the company" work that would usually be handled by an elite large law firm. Typically, these independent secondment firms charge on a weekly flat fee basis, in direct response to clients' expressed need for more predictability in their budgets. The secondment firms will often hire the lawyers as W-2 employees and provide benefits to them to work on-site at their clients' offices. This meets many clients' preferences to eliminate the associated risk of hiring an employee. Clients also like the model when they anticipate that the need will be temporary, or that the need might be there indefinitely, but they are not authorized to increase headcount. In a typical secondment, when the project ends, so does the attorney's engagement with the company.

While the notion of temporary or contract lawyers, as they are sometimes called, is not new, what is different today is the nature of services these lawyers provide, the types of lawyers who are engaging in secondment work, and their compensation and treatment as W-2 employees. A seconded lawyer today is usually a well-credentialed, experienced lawyer receiving full benefits whose average staffing at a particular company runs about a year. Many seconded lawyers like the flexibility of being staffed on a variety of matters for different clients with the freedom to accept or decline an assignment to work instead with a new client in a new industry, or to take time off for personal reasons, giving them greater flexibility than the traditional legal model ever afforded.

The profile of the seconded lawyer varies considerably and has evolved over time. The demographic ranges from a parent who wants more flexibility in his or her schedule, to a lawyer at the other end of his or her career arc who is less concerned with building a résumé but would like to remain engaged in selective work before retiring. Re-entry mothers who have left the profession for a time and are seeking to return are among the available talent pool for secondments, as are lawyers who have been laid-off or are otherwise in transition who can jump in immediately on a pressing project that may arise. The secondee talent pool is also comprised of law firm lawyers who have been trying to transition to an in-house role for a number of years but cannot seem to gain entry without in-house experience. Some are willing to take a long-term temporary engagement in order to hopefully become a permanent employee at the in-house legal department where they are engaged or at a future one. These law firm lawyers have found that the risk in making this choice to explore a temporary in-house role has ultimately been less than they might have thought. Often, their law firm employers are providing open offers to return, with the thought that the returning lawyer might also be able to bring a new client back to the firm.

There are some limits to the secondment model. Ideally, seconded lawyers will embody the autonomy that the model provides and revel in the opportunity to accept or decline the next engagement when a prior assignment ends. However, just as a law firm cannot guarantee a certain type of substantive work that a lawyer prefers, there is no guarantee that the next engagement that perfectly suits a seconded lawyer will appear at the right time. While many lawyers thrive on the flexibility that such a model creates, the inherent lack of security of temporary engagements are stressful for some who prefer that the temporary position evolves into a permanent role—which happens at times, but not in the majority of cases.

A related concern for potential secondees is the lack of continuity that their resumes may reflect if they engage in multiple secondments for different clients over several years. We find that this concern is become increasingly minimized, however, with the evolution of the legal marketplace. Employers recognize that lawyers today have less longevity in their places of employment and with that comes reduced expectations of long-term work commitments. Additionally, most secondees are experienced lawyers who have formerly held jobs at more traditional firms and companies so when they list on their resume an overall consulting title with bullets reflecting different engagements for various clients, it can add another dimension to a candidate's resume and serve to enhance the breadth of a candidate's appeal.

Another secondment challenge arises when a secondee feels like a second-class citizen at a company. Corporate culture plays an important role in the success of secondments. Some companies embrace the secondee as an integral contributor, while other companies are not as well versed in or experienced at valuing temporary members of the team. Those legal departments with the most success are the ones that are built on bringing in secondees on a temporary basis and then converting them to permanent employees after ensuring that the secondees have both the requisite skill set and the cultural fit. Peter Piazza, Senior Vice President and General Counsel of Commercial Transactions at The Nielsen Company, has helped to establish a culture of respect and collaboration that embraces all of their secondees as full members of the team without distinction. All of Peter's secondees are included at firm meetings, company off-site retreats, and are given access to high-quality work on the basis of merit. This level of inclusiveness and thoughtful integration are steps that other in-house leaders can emulate to remedy some secondees' feelings of a diminished status and in turn, increase the contribution and value that secondees can bring.

While secondments originated with attorneys filling various temporary spots in companies as the needs arose, these roles have expanded. In one managed services model, for example, lawyers and non-lawyer professionals are brought on temporarily to work offsite and as a group to tackle large projects for a company for an extended term. There are also tiers of secondment firms, attracting various levels of talent depending on how appealing they find the client engagements, compensation packages and anticipated lifestyle. Secondment clients have also expanded to include traditional law firms, as well as in-house legal departments, as will be more fully explored below.

There can be no discussion of secondment firms without acknowledging the important innovation of Mark Harris in founding the company Axiom. In addition to creating a new legal model in which lawyers could practice law differently, Harris responded to clients' need for predictability by charging a weekly fixed fee and also significantly reducing companies' outside counsel spend by providing an alternative source for talent. Since Axiom's founding, many other secondment firms have emerged and created variations of these secondment offerings.

THE COMBINED VIRTUAL AND SECONDMENT FIRM

While we have touted the benefits of virtual and secondment firms, we think that even greater benefits emerge from the combination of the virtual and secondment firm innovations. That being said, we need to disclose that, to our knowledge, the only firm that has combined these innovations is our own Bliss Lawyers. So as we recognize that this content may be construed as shameless self-promotion, we hope you will indulge us because we also believe that the combined virtual and secondment firm illustrates an important part of the innovation story that we are seeking to tell in this chapter.

By their nature, secondment firms typically charge about one-third to one half of what large law firms charge (which is also in line with the rates charged by virtual law firms). If a firm delivers secondment services from a virtual platform, however, not only do the clients receive more competitive pricing but also the savings is not created at the expense of the lawyer's salary or benefits. By eliminating the real estate costs of a bricks and mortar office, a combined virtual and secondment firm is able to offer the generous compensation that attracts high-caliber talent while still delivering cost savings to its clients.

There are many talented attorneys who are still displaced as a result of the economic downturn. The opportunities provided through a secondment in an in-house legal department have become a way for this talent pool to return to their desired career trajectory. Bliss has seen this play out when it hired Jason Nussbaum, a junior attorney who graduated from Fordham Law School in 2010. Jason had earned a sought-after summer associate position at one of New York City's most prestigious large law firms. Unfortunately, in 2009, in response to the economic downturn, this firm did not extend offers to a large portion of its summer associate class. Instead of beginning his career at a large law firm as planned, Jason's intended path was derailed as a result of circumstances beyond his control. Bliss hired him to work in-house at a large investment bank, and in 2012 the client directly hired him as counsel and his career is back on track. This example demonstrates the value of extracting different learnings from various innovations and blending models, where possible.

Thus, at Bliss Lawyers, we learned from combining the secondment and virtual models, but we also learned the value of adjusting our model to facilitate a direct hire. We have found that both clients and lawyers often express a desire to transition to more permanent hiring solutions after a temporary engagement. From the in-house vantage point, this may be due to a change in headcount authorization, or a growing and unanticipated work need, or otherwise. We have seen that clients also enjoy availing themselves of the opportunity to put into place what we call an "extended interview." By engaging lawyers temporarily initially, clients can ensure that a lawyer's work quality is up to par and that he or she fits into the corporate culture. Clients anticipate that this trial period will result in better employment decisions for the company as well as the lawyer in the long run. What this example speaks to in the larger sense is that innovation is not fixed. In other words, once an innovation is implemented, the work does not stop there. Real innovation requires a constant assessment of market needs and resultant responsiveness to the ever changing demands.

NONTRADITIONAL LAW FIRMS

Another innovation underway is from those firms that have initiated an alternative to how they bill for their services. Some small- to medium-size firms have looked long and hard at the billable hour and have come up with alternative fee structures for the more predictable work they perform. While the concept of alternative fees is not new, what is different is that some firms have emerged as exclusive alternative fee firms, marketing themselves as providing legal services based on other measures than the billable hour. Valorem Law Group is one such firm that has focused on the concept of value and has created the Value Adjustment Line: In each bill, Valorem includes its agreed upon fee with the client as well as a space for the client to make any adjustment the client deems necessary.

Another such firm founded on the alternative fee premise is Australia's Marque Lawyers. It charges clients by a fixed periodic fee (usually monthly) under either a global retainer covering all of their legal work or a specific retainer covering identified aspects of the work. The fee has no carve-outs or exclusions, and it can include litigation in the retainer at the clients' preference. The retainer fee is regularly reviewed to ensure fairness. Such alternative fee firms like Valorem and Marque Lawyers have been successful in distinguishing themselves in the market as offering an alternative to traditional lawyering, thereby creating a different type of relationship with their clients.

EVOLVED TRADITIONAL LAW FIRMS

Each of the new model firms and legal service providers described here owes a debt of gratitude to traditional law firms. Without law firms performing the crucial function of training junior lawyers, many of the innovative new legal models would not be possible. Additionally, many of the innovations in new model firms have been developed directly in response to the flaws and inefficiencies of the traditional law firm model.

In the past, the traditional law firm infrastructure as well as the partnership model combined with lawyers' historic risk aversion have interfered with the innovation of many firms. However, the volatile market and stagnant growth have set the stage for traditional law firms to innovate too. Thus, the traditional law firm innovations are largely attributable to market pressures, the success of new legal models, and the ability of traditional firms to identify their own inefficiencies more critically. In turn, Debbie has observed that other than innovation in billing that will be more fully explored in later chapters, traditional law firm innovations are chiefly taking place in three respects: the talent pool, the use of space and the categorization of information. Here are some examples of innovation unfolding in traditional law firm models.

Rethinking the Talent Pool

We have been struck by the number of U.K. firms that have developed their own flexible, resourcing model to compete with the secondment and smaller or new model firms whose rates are more competitive and predictable. Berwin Leighton Paisner (BLP), a U.K. firm, created Lawyers on Demand (LOD) in 2008. A fixed pool of temporary, freelance lawyers who are vetted and supported on a contract basis work with the firm's clients handling projects at a discount.

In 2011, the law firm Eversheds launched Agile to provide temporary, vetted professionals for those who desire Eversheds's experience and resources without wanting to commit to a long-term engagement. The law firm Freshfields Bruckhaus Deringer created Freshfields Continuum in 2012 as a means to use their alumni network to provide more competitive pricing on a project basis to its clients. By pricing work at four rates, Freshfields is using a talent pool that has already been vetted to service its clients' evolving, cost-conscious needs. In 2013, the law firm of Pinsent Masons LLP's opened its own freelance lawyer service, Vario, which similarly provides a pool of freelance legal professionals for clients to use when needed, allowing clients to access quality legal services at a lower cost. Also in 2013, Allen & Overy, another firm in the U.K. legal market, launched a flexible resourcing business called Peerpoint where it employs its alumni on a contract basis to supplement its permanent workforce at times of high demand or to provide specialist skills support. Other flexible resourcing businesses launched by legal practices recently include DAC Beachcroft's The People Pool, which provides human resources and employment specialists with access to DAC Beachcroft's partners to work on temporary engagements. Similarly, Transatlantic Law International's Labor Law Plus has regional teams around the globe that can supply experienced legal professionals for temporary, fixed cost engagements.

In the U.S., traditional law firms have not generally been as focused on developing their own temporary talent pool. An exception is Fenwick & West LLP—it developed a consulting service of what it calls FLEX attorneys, a stable of high-caliber attorneys who work at predictable rates. FLEX clients purchase blocks of legal counsel time—in weekly or quarterly chunks—and use their allotment as they see fit. These FLEX attorneys respond not only to Fenwick & West's clients' interest in lower rates but also to their desire for predictability.

While it is a necessity that traditional law firms innovate to avoid losing business in an increasingly competitive global market, Debbie wonders whether law firms' efforts to create temporary talent pools will ultimately become another means of inefficiency. Rather than have each large firm develop its own internal resource model, would it not be more efficient, cost effective and consistent with the outsourcing trends in the market to contract out this service and manage it instead? While we readily admit that this is a self-interested point, we think it is an issue of importance to the innovation discussion, as Bliss has seen this question increasingly play out with U.S. law firms. Here's how: While we conceived of our secondment firm to respond to in-house legal department needs, Bliss opened a law firm division in 2014 to also service law firms. We did this in direct response to what we believe to be an increased law firm understanding that the employment risk, coupled with the task of identifying, cultivating and vetting the right talent pool to service its clients, is an onerous burden and one that may be better met through an outside source.

The realization that it may be more cost-efficient and less cumbersome to outsource the temporary pool of lawyers is compounded by the recognition that secondment firms exclusively focused on this service, given the volume, can deliver it at a higher quality and with greater efficiency. Additionally, traditional firms need to be mindful of their image and not run the risk of having clients demand lower prices and predictability across the board for all of their services. While it appears that traditional firms have anticipated this issue by separately branding their flexible sourcing initiatives, it remains to be seen whether traditional firms' efforts to service both needs ultimately will tarnish their reputation or diminish their ability to simultaneously command high rates and perform traditional legal work.

Thus, the long-term sustainability of large law firm innovation in the temporary talent space remains in question. However, we believe that temporary and contract lawyers are not going away. Indeed, in Altman Weil's 2014 Law Firms in Transition survey, 72 percent of the interviewed managing partners and chairs believed that the increased use of contract lawyers was a permanent change in the legal market.[20]

Another opportunity for innovation in the use of talent in traditional law firms may be in lawyers not practicing law at all and in the increased use of non-lawyer professionals. This was one of the findings of Law 2023, a group of thought leaders that spent a year evaluating law firm trends in technology, economics and cultural change and concluded with seven rules of "how today's firms can prosper from the coming disruption."[21] In an explanation of Rule Four: "Firms will tap new talent and enable new pathways to practice", Law 2023 predicts that "jobs like project manager and client service manager will become increasingly prevalent. New positions such as programmer, business analyst, industry advisor, etc. could be filled either by lawyers or professionals with other backgrounds."[22]

---

20. Thomas S. Clay and Eric A. Seeger, 2014 Law Firms In Transition: An Altman Weil Flash Survey, 2014.
21. Law 2023, "Findings," at http://www.law2023.org/.
22. Ibid. at http://www.law2023.org/rule-4; *see also* Richard Susskind, *Tomorrow's Lawyers: An Introduction to Your Future* (Oxford: Oxford University Press, 2013).

Reengineering the Use of Space

Some firms have focused less on reengineering the talent pool and more on reengineering the space or some combination of the two. One notable example was in 2010, when CMS Cameron McKenna signed a £583 million ($974,927,580) outsourcing agreement with Integreon. The goal was to create a shared service center that was to provide business support services and an information technology infrastructure. Although the contract was supposed to cover a ten-year period, in 2013 the firm announced that it would scale back its agreement with Integreon.

In the U.S., the notion of reengineering law firm office space is gaining traction. Previously, what this meant was firms including WilmerHale; Bingham McCutchen; Orrick, Herrington & Sutcliffe; Pillsbury Winthrop Shaw Pittman and others relocating their respective business operations to less expensive regions of the country to reduce their real estate costs as a way to be more price competitive. Other firms remodeled their offices to create consolidated public conference rooms and lounges separated from the rest of the law office or redesigned their conference center in a bid to increase productivity and maximize use of available space. Additionally, Greenberg Traurig LLP was a leader in renewing the lease of its sizeable Miami office to save on costs by building a smaller office that was designed for more lawyers.[23] Greenberg designed an impressive centralized conference floor where clients would visit and more modest smaller offices and communal work spaces for the other floors.[24]

Firms are now thinking more broadly about reengineering space, as reflected in a 2014 American Bar Association (ABA) Journal article that featured three top trends among law firms to address the "challenges involving space usage, costs and culture: glass-walled

---

23. Deborah Epstein Henry, *Law & Reorder: Legal Industry Solutions for Restructure, Retention, Promotion & Work/Life Balance* (Chicago: American Bar Association, 2010): 206.
24. Ibid.

interiors, hospitality industry touches and amazing eating spaces."[25] The "glass-walled interiors" refers to using glass and natural light to illuminate the space, make connections with colleagues easier and make the office seem larger as well as more active, high energy and collaborative. To address privacy and glare concerns, shade and frosted glass are used.[26] "Hospitality industry touches" connotes making the law firm feel more like the style of a boutique hotel that is both comfortable and professional.[27] Additionally, "amazing eating spaces" allow firms to create a culture and a forum for greater collegiality and collaboration.[28] These efforts are aligned with bringing down real estate costs by creating more communal areas and better use of space and light to reduce square footage.

Reconfiguring the Categorization of Information

Law firms have also begun to innovate in the categorization of information. One fitting example is what Morgan, Lewis & Bockius LLP has done in creating its eData Practice that was developed in direct response to the reality that most corporate business information is now in electronic form, and many companies are struggling to manage increasingly large volumes of data. Morgan Lewis's eData Practice works with clients' in-house legal and information technology teams to create customized records-management systems that reduce regulatory and litigation risks, streamline discovery processes, and cost effectively serve each company's long-term business objectives. Morgan Lewis's focus on alternative billing and creating efficiencies with respect to its eData Practice is a means to preempt the alternative sources that clients would entertain if such a service were not provided. Jones Day and Perkins Coie, among

---

25. Jenny B. Davis, "Designing Your Law Office to Save Money and Boost Productivity—Without Sacrificing Style" *ABA Journal*, July 2014, http://www.abajournal.com/magazine/article/designing_your_law_office_to_save_money_and_boost_productivity/.
26. Ibid.
27. Ibid.
28. Ibid.

other firms, have also focused on developing more efficient e-discovery practices through devoted e-discovery services.

HYBRID INNOVATION

In some cases, innovation is being driven by a combination of approaches. One example is Riverview Law, a partially DLA Piper-backed fixed-fee legal services company that aligned with U.K. law firm DHM Stallard about a year after its founding. The model offers businesses monthly contracts for all of their day-to-day legal support, or they can receive a fixed price quote for a specific piece of work. Additionally, large companies can outsource their in-house legal function to Riverview Law for a fixed price. The alliance with DHM Stallard is a means to attract more notable clients who may still be seeking a name brand and traditional model and combining that with the fresh insights of a new legal model that is more agile with respect to alternative fee arrangements.

Hybrid innovation is also underway with new model firms that enter the market with one innovation, say secondments, and then venture into other areas of growth like outsourcing, document review, etc. Technology is often one of the key drivers that allows these new models to expand from one type of work to another. At Bliss, we consider ourselves hybrid innovators, having combined two innovations—the secondment and virtual models—at the outset. This spirit continues as we regularly evaluate the demands of the market. Along these lines, market demands and the learnings of recruiting firms that allow temporary lawyers to convert into permanent employees assisted us in extending that option to our clients and lawyers as well.

Hybrid innovation does not come without its challenges. As new model firms branch out into different areas, they need to be mindful of not diluting their brand and having their expansion efforts backfire. The pacing and breadth of growth for new model firms is even more important than that of traditional ones, given that new model firms are already less familiar in the market.

CONCLUSION

As we have explored innovations in the legal field, what we have learned from our meetings with general counsel and law firm management, as well as our research and observation of market trends, is that we really are talking about process. By process, we mean the actual conceptualization, performance, and delivery of the legal work. We believe that innovation in law may ultimately hinge on those who are most insightful about anticipating the next process that will be needed and how, ultimately, that process will be executed in the most cost-effective way without compromising the quality of the end product.

Part of that process undoubtedly will require a greater project management infrastructure at each stage of a representation. This role goes beyond the mastery of reasoning and it becomes about the cost-effective, efficient, high-quality and seamless execution of the work as well. Those who develop the means to efficiently and expertly direct and execute the workflow, both within a legal department and outside of it, will be the ones who win out in shaping the future of law and the profession.

2

VALUE

I regard the law firms working on my most important matters as respected strategic partners. Our work together has been and has to be mutually beneficial. While I am invested in the strong relationships I have built with these firms, I am not focused on their business models. My job as a General Counsel is to obsess over my company's business and given those demands, there is not much room to worry about the issues facing other businesses.

Law firms have been struggling to recreate themselves for two decades, well longer than the most recent business contraction so frequently cited as the reason for the "paradigm shift" allegedly underway. I believe the billable hour is at the root of many law firm challenges.

This chapter succinctly lays out the deleterious effects of the hourly rate on a General Counsel's perception of the value of law firm legal services, including an exploration of alternative

Continued

RANDAL MILCH, EXECUTIVE VICE PRESIDENT AND GENERAL COUNSEL, VERIZON *CONTINUED*

fee arrangements and the importance of aligning law firm and client interests. This chapter also provides a set of structural solutions aimed at increasing the value of law firm services. Perhaps there is hope after all.

INTRODUCTION

Gone are the days when a law department was the only department in a company that did not need a budget. Also gone are the days when a large bill could be mailed with a note to a client: "For Services Rendered" with the expectation that the client would pay by return mail. Clients have grown increasingly sophisticated and now require not only transparency and collaboration from their outside counsel but often predictability in budgets as well. Many clients no longer accept that a firm that has handled, for example, breach of contract cases for the past 30 years cannot effectively predict the cost of a new breach of contract case, particularly when reasonable ranges and checkpoints can be incorporated into a budget. When law firms fail to take the initiative to develop creative alternatives, but instead hold on to the sacred cow of the billable hour, it leads to a diminished trust between client and law firm, threatening to derail the increasingly tenuous advisory relationship.

Developed in the 1950's when lawyers felt they were losing economic ground to doctors,[1] the billable hour today has often become a battleground where law firms and clients stand in direct conflict. The paradox is this: In order for a law firm that operates

---

1. Adam Liptak, "Stop the Clock? Critics Call the Billable Hour a Legal Fiction," N.Y. Times, Oct. 29, 2002, http://www.nytimes.com/2002/10/29/jobs/on-the-job-s top-the-clock-critics-call-the-billable-hour-a-legal-fiction.html.

on the billable hour model to become most profitable, it must do its work as inefficiently as possible—to the detriment of the client. However, the paradox is not that simple. Law firms know that clients do not want to pay more than what an efficient operation would require. The only way they will get repeat business and not lose a client or face unbearable pressure to cut rates is if they are careful about the hours that they bill. Additionally, while clients outwardly resent the billable hour model, they too frequently default to it as the devil they know. The alternatives are unfamiliar and often cumbersome, while the billable hour enables clients to most readily compare competing outside counsel.

In March 2009, during the peak of the global downturn, the billable hour came under increasing scrutiny when the Association of Corporate Counsel (ACC) issued The Value Challenge. The ACC convened a summit of in-house counsel from some of the world's 20 largest corporations and partners from 20 major law firms to address the subject of controlling legal costs—and also to encourage the legal profession to think differently about how to deliver value.

During this same time period, Debbie posited that among the future challenges to the profession would be measuring value as it manifests in three respects—the value of a matter, the value of a lawyer's contribution and the value of a law firm.[2] Assessing the value of a matter involves determining a measure, other than billable hours, to evaluate what it will cost to handle a representation for a client. Assessing the value of a lawyer means determining what a lawyer's contribution is both internally—as a team member to be evaluated and promoted—as well as externally—to determine what to bill the client for that lawyer's work on a matter. Assessing the value of a law firm means assessing the success of a law firm other than by profits per equity partner.[3] While important progress has

---

2. Deborah Epstein Henry, *Law & Reorder: Legal Industry Solutions for Restructure, Retention, Promotion & Work/Life Balance* (Chicago, American Bar Association, 2010): 51–52.
3. Ibid.

been made in defining value, alternative approaches have not taken hold at the same pace as one would think. So here we explore the pressing questions posed: How do we fairly and accurately value a matter, a lawyer and a law firm?

HOW DO WE VALUE A MATTER?

While the hope had been that the increased focus spurred by ACC's Value Challenge would accelerate creative alternative fee arrangements, the reality is that lawyers continue to struggle to find meaningful ways to value a matter other than the billable hour. Beginning in 1989, when the ABA launched the Law Practice Management Section Task Force on Alternative Billing Methods, the legal profession has been in a self-exploratory process to determine new ways to bill clients.[4] In turn, there is a long overdue response to determine a way to bill for services that is consistent with how most other businesses operate.

When observing how law firms interact with others who deliver professional services, interestingly, the billable hour is often not the dominant governing means. When law firms hire outside consultants, for example, they typically do so because of the analysis and/or result the consultants will deliver and the expertise that they bring. While law firms are at times billed hourly for that work, e.g., an expert witness, firms often do not expect to be billed by the number of hours the consultants spend on the project. Instead, they focus on the delivered result rather than the cost and time it took to achieve the result.

Common sense dictates then that when a client hires a lawyer to handle a representation, the lawyer's time and effort is typically not determinative for the client. In Debbie's experience, she has found that what truly matters to a client in determining the appropriate

---

4. ABA Commission on Billable Hours. "ABA Commission on Billable Hours Report 2001–2002" (Chicago: American Bar Association, 2002): vii.

lawyer to handle a matter or in assessing a lawyer's performance is three factors—what she calls the Value Measure:

- Efficiency
- Quality of Work
- Results Achieved

Looking at these three in turn can form the basis for an alternative fee arrangement. Efficiency measures how quickly the work can be performed while not compromising the quality of the service provided. Quality of Work maintains that the work is performed at a certain standard of excellence. Results Achieved, or impact, assesses the overall result or deliverable of the work. Results Achieved is thus differentiated from Quality of Work where, for example, a representation was conducted efficiently, and with great acumen—yet the result was still unfavorable to the client. This is not meant to suggest that a law firm can be held solely accountable for a client's loss. A law firm is constrained by the facts presented, the other parties to the matter, as well as market trends and fluctuations. However, the firm can and should be evaluated, at least in part, based on what it does with the facts at hand and how it makes the most of the circumstances provided.

Thus, to bring real value to the profession, the three factors—Efficiency, Quality of Work, and Results Achieved—need to be the focus so that law firms are not operating on principles that run counter to the client's interest. These factors are what make business sense and, therefore, they need to be the factors at play to determine how a representation is billed.

One simple example of how the Value Measure can best be applied is a flat or project fee with a bonus component. This alternative fee arrangement provides a way to value a matter using a measure other than time. While law firm lawyers often resist the notion that they should be able to estimate an appropriate project fee, experienced practitioners should be able to give a reasonable estimate in most circumstances. Take the breach of contract case we mentioned earlier: An experienced litigator should be able to anticipate a series of outcomes and likelihoods in order to provide a range of reasonable fees for each stage of a litigation. While there are certain categories of litigation where such a project fee would be more challenging due to the unpredictable nature of that practice area, many types of matters could more readily fit within this approach.

Often what prevents law firms from engaging in alternative fee arrangements—especially for the first time—is the fear that they will underestimate the time expended on a representation and, if they are wrong, the firm will lose significant revenue from the representation. This is when communication become important. It is in both the client's and the law firm's interest to allow for regular check-ins regarding the price of a representation because variables can play out both ways; unexpected contingencies may result to the detriment of the client and/or the law firm.

Unit pricing, which sets one fee for each stage of a transaction or proceeding, can also be an effective means to ensure dialogue between the law firm and the client if the expectations at any stage of the transaction or proceeding are inconsistent with what unfolds. In turn, unit pricing is a means to bring fairness and address the reticence that many law firms have in engaging in alternative fees. However, it comes with a note of caution. When unit pricing results in firms falling back on the billable hour to figure out if the time spent by its lawyers is fairly allocated, then it leads to the circular problem of relying on the billable hour as the value determinant rather than another metric.

While the flat or project fee provides the predictability that a client needs in adhering to a legal budget, such a fee alone is not enough to align the law firm and client interests. To really engage the law firm to be as incentivized as its client, a bonus component should be included in the alternative fee arrangement. The bonus serves as a way for the law firm to participate in the representation as the client's true partner by providing a financial reward if a law firm achieves a favorable outcome for the client—whether that be a speedier result, a favorable settlement, a win at trial or some other predetermined measure of success. Some find the notion that lawyers would need bonuses to enhance their efforts for clients to be offensive. However, these bonuses should be perceived not as necessary motivation for a firm to do good work but rather as recognition that the firm is accepting front-end risk and therefore should share in back-end rewards.

Another benefit to providing a bonus for a firm's work is that it encourages the firm to discuss the client's goals before the representation begins. While understanding a client's goals may seem like an obvious part of the initial strategy, often there are a number of intentions that are not otherwise identified until later on in a representation. This effort to articulate and align a law firm and client's interests at the beginning will more likely result in the law firm understanding and directly pursuing its clients' goals from the outset.

The combined flat and bonus fee is just one example of an alternative fee arrangement that provides the Value Measure. To assess other viable options, the same three factors of Efficiency, Quality of Work, and Results Achieved would need to be applied to determine if an alternative fee arrangement is designed in such a way that a law firm can effectively deliver legal services for a reasonable fee to the satisfaction of the client.

While we believe the Value Measure is the best means to meet today's legal services' needs, this is not to suggest that there is no continuing role for the billable hour in the marketplace. In fact, Garry has found that in running Berger Legal, his clients often prefer the billable hour when securing his services. Perhaps his clients have found that once they experience the inherent discounts that are built into the virtual firm model, they are less likely to pursue the value question in another realm.

Along these lines, an in-house lawyer from a prominent financial services company found himself faced with a need to handle a large volume of repeat workflow of certain time sensitive matters and coordinated with Berger Legal to develop a cost-effective solution to meet their needs. Suzie explains that in circumstances such as this, Berger Legal clients often prefer creating a cap for certain types of workflows. In turn, the billable hour is used as a benchmark to anticipate the average amount of time that a volume of work will take, creating predictability for their clients and having Berger Legal share some of the risk. This serves as an effective solution for high volume, time sensitive work often referred to as "short fuse workflows" to meet the needs of certain financial services clients. The result was a favorable solution that solved a pressing need for this in-house legal department.

HOW DO WE VALUE AN ATTORNEY?

When we look at the three factors that determine the value of a representation for purposes of an alternative fee arrangement—Efficiency, Quality of Work, and Results Achieved—we see that these same measures can be applied to assess the contribution of a law firm lawyer. Currently, most law firms rely heavily on hours logged in evaluating associates for promotion considerations.

Let's take Associate A at a large New York City law firm who bills 1,900 hours a year. He is consistently rated as performing high-quality work. Associate B, on the other hand, bills 2,400 hours a year—which entitles her to receive a higher bonus and provides her with an easier trajectory to partnership elevation. From one perspective this makes sense: the law firm makes money when an associate delivers billable hours, and Associate B is generating more revenue for the firm. From another perspective, this seems absurd: just because Associate B is willing to log the hours—does that mean she is more bonus-eligible and promotion-ready than Associate A? Or does it simply mean that Associate A is more efficient than his colleague? We might say that if Associate B were not really that good, then she would not be getting the work; sub-par lawyers are never this busy because no one in the firm wants to use them. Additionally, in logging the extra hours, Associate B has the opportunity to gain more substantive experience and expo-sure. Fair enough. But if Associate A and Associate B produce the same volume and quality of work and achieve the same results, should law firms really value Associate B more highly because she takes more time to achieve the same outcome? There need to be additional measures to value associates other than through bill-able hours. Otherwise, hours logged turns into years logged, thus leading to a promotion-by-inertia model, which overvalues time and undervalues skill, proficiency, and impact—all of which are ultimately more responsive to client needs.

As it stands now, in many law firms, associate progression is established nearly by rote. Every year, on September 1, an associ-ate's seniority goes up. Associates go from first year to second year, nearly automatically—and it is often not until lawyers are in their fifth year or later, before getting some real feedback about whether they would realistically be considered for partner. While, we are over-simplifying the process, the point is that this general law firm progression exists nowhere else in corporate America: You are a year older, so you get your next promotion. If this approach were limited to the internal workings of a law firm, it might be sustain-able. However, the internal process is mirrored by the parallel rate increases applied to clients each year an associate becomes elevated. What has happened since the economic downturn, though, is that clients have started pushing back; they are getting smarter. They are resisting a law firm's inclination to increase rates unless the law firm can show an associates's demonstrated knowledge gained or improvement in the services delivered.

It was at this time, when clients started pushing back, that some law firms began actively introducing the concept of core compe-tencies. Rather than calling their lawyers third- or seventh-year associates, some law firms established three levels for their associates: junior-level, mid-level and senior-level. In addition to establishing core competencies required of everyone who worked at the firm, such as the ability to be a good writer, a good communicator, etc., separate competencies were established based on each practice area. To be a junior associate litigator, for example, you might have to have written a series of motions, or defended a certain number of depositions, or have written a variety of briefs before you could progress to the next level.

Critics at the time said that the implementation of core competencies was a ruse used by law firms during the economic downturn to avoid raising their lawyers' salaries, as associates now had to meet additional criteria in order to get promoted and receive a raise in earnings. However, the establishment of core competencies, when properly implemented, is a committed approach to defining value both internally at firms and externally for clients. Rather than simply having a fifth-year associate staffed on a particular matter and paying the fifth-year associate rate, ideally clients would now be serviced by the work of a mid-level associate whom they knew was capable of delivering the skills required for that particular representation, thereby justifying the work being billed out at a certain rate.

Many firms that implemented core competency models have since retreated from them. For some firms, the subjectivity of applying core competencies and the difficulty of fairly and consistently assessing benchmarks has been problematic. For law firms that have retained core competencies, the challenge of determining compensation remains. Ideally, with a new talent management system and associated billing structure, a new process would also have been implemented to determine pay scale and promotions. However, in reality, when firms actually got around to evaluating promotions and bonuses at the end of the year, they fell back on what they knew: the billable hour. Core competencies are an important piece of the puzzle of determining value, but thus far they have not ultimately become the Value Measure. As with finding a new measure to value a representation or matter, the challenge remains to categorically change the way we measure an associate's contribution without principally falling back on the measure of time.

STRATIFICATION OF THE LEGAL TALENT POOL AS A NEW MEANS TO ESTABLISH VALUE

While it has proven difficult to measure a law firm lawyer's value other than by time spent, the billable hour alone is not to blame. Another factor contributing to the challenge is the traditional law firm career path. For many years, the law firm model was based on the premise that everyone aspired to become an equity partner—defined by the American Lawyer as those who receive no more than half their compensation on a fixed-income basis.[5] Historically, becoming an equity partner has been attractive to those who want to become a part owner in a business and to share in the profits. Many have also aspired to become equity partners because equity partners hold the power in law firms to vote on governing law firm and other strategic business decisions.

But not everyone who joins a law firm wants to make equity partner. In fact, the trend shows that fewer and fewer attorneys are seeking that level of ownership and responsibility.[6] Increasingly, there are lawyers who recognize that in exchange for the money and power, often the equity partner needs to sacrifice his or her weekends, vacations, and sleep. When equity partnership meant significant financial security and stature, many were eager to assume this path. However, on top of lifestyle tradeoffs, today the hope of

---

5. For purposes of discussion, the *American Lawyer* definitions of "Equity Partner" and "Non-Equity Partner" are being used herein, "Our Methodology," *American Lawyer*, modified on April 28, 2014, http://www.americanlawyer.com/id=1202652499623.
6. David Behrend; "Sacrifices to Becoming a Partner in a Large Law Firm." *Lexis-Nexis Legal NewsRoom, Career Guidance*, November 4, 2012; Janet Ellen Raasch, "Making Partner—Or Not Is It In, Up or Over in the 21st Century?" *33 Law Prac.* 32 (2007), http://www.americanbar.org/publications/law_practice_home/law_practice_archive/lpm_magazine_articles_v33_is4_an1.html.

financial security and power is riddled with serious risk. In turn, the lure of equity partnership has diminished for many.

SWAPPING OUT THE BRASS RING

There is a stark disconnect between the path that most associates purport to desire and the path that many associates actually want to pursue at law firms. Not everyone wants the potential risk of equity partnership or the investment that firms often require through capital contributions. Some are unwilling to spend their evenings pitching business and developing their marketing profile. There are others who fear that if they become an equity partner, they will be owned by their work which is not a sacrifice they are willing to make. Many individuals, for a whole host of reasons, want more predictability and control in their scheduling. They want to know when they are leaving work and when they need to be on call. They are unwilling to cancel their vacations.

Beyond the issues of "want," many law firm lawyers are not cut out for the equity partner role, even if they were willing to put in the time. What's more is that the law firm model does not support that everyone become an equity partner, hence the "up and out" approach to law firm promotions for associates who cannot meet the demands of the equity partnership path. This would then seem to be a self-contained problem because while the promotion opportunities are not there for everyone, the desire and talent are not there either. However, the problem is not self-contained. Instead, the fallacy of most lawyers being put on the equity partner track remains, and the alternatives provided for those who are not on track often stigmatize the lawyers who seek them. In short, there needs to be valued alternative career paths for practicing lawyers at law firms.

What if someone does not want the brass ring or does not have the skill set to achieve it? We believe that equity partner should not be the only valued role in law firms. Every law firm lawyer wants to take pride in his or her work. Additionally, from the law firm's perspective, in order to inspire the best work from a lawyer, that lawyer must be happy, engaged, and valued.

Debbie proposes an alternative value solution—to swap out the brass ring for five Olympic rings. Rather than a single ring designating one celebrated path to equity partner (that many are either unfit for or do not want to pursue), she suggests that one consider the Olympic logo instead. With its five intertwined rings—each a different color, the Olympic image represents five different career paths to pursue with associated promotion paths and titles to achieve.

In the Olympics, there are definitive awards that athletes aspire to obtain: a gold, silver, and bronze medal. Similarly, in the five rings of career paths, there would be milestones and titles recognizing the various levels of promotions within each career path. Importantly, for those on each career path who do not achieve these highest levels of achievement—the medals, if you will—a talent management decision would be made to determine whether they would still be valued members of the team or if they no longer make the cut to compete.

In the law firm context, here's how the Olympic Rings of Talent might play out as a means of providing five valued career paths, including the equity partner path. Note that different firms may use different terms than the ones provided below; this should nonetheless provide a framework for a broader discussion around creating multiple valued career paths to success.

Junior Associate; Senior Associate; Equity Partner

These are lawyers who start their career as junior associates. These junior associates are well-credentialed and capable not only of doing the work but also of being fully engaged in developing their careers. In addition to doing the substantive work, these associates are involved in the firm by serving on committees. They develop their external profile by getting involved in the community, trade associations or bar associations, and by perhaps writing articles or giving presentations to build their visibility. Their progression continues as they are promoted to senior associates. The next step for the senior associates is equity partnership unless the firm has a mandatory first step to non-equity partnership (defined by the *American Lawyer* as those who receive more than half their compensation on a fixed basis[7]). As non-equity partners on a path to be equity partners or as equity partners already, these lawyers would continue to deliver on the work and demonstrate the ability to generate client relationships and originate business for the firm.

Junior Associate; Senior Associate; Non-Equity Partner

There are two types of lawyers who may take the non-equity partner path. One group is comprised of the same junior associates and senior associates described in the equity partner path; becoming a non-equity partner is thus a stepping stone to being made full equity partner. The other type of lawyers start out on the junior associate path but pursue the non-equity partner title and do not seek to transition to equity partner. This may be because they do not have the business development skills required, and they are not interested in or effective at cultivating them, or it may be that they do not want to devote the extra time and commitment to what the equity partner role entails. Non-equity partners may also not want to assume the associated investment and/or risk that is required of equity partners.

Non-Equity Partner; Equity Partner; Senior Counsel

This path might be assumed by those who have previously held the role of non-equity partner or equity partner. For those who are getting close to retirement, this recognized path reflects the firm prioritizing the value of partners building a legacy and being able to effectively transition their relationships and their knowledge. These

---

7. "Our Methodology," American Lawyer, modified on April 28, 2014, http://www .americanlawyer.com/id=1202652499623.

respected lawyers typically have strong client relationships, but they are no longer interested in billing the demanding hours they once did. Or, they may be interested in focusing more on mentoring or sponsoring junior lawyers, as they phase out of practice, perhaps on a flexible or reduced hours basis. Valuing this role has become particularly important in light of today's disproportionately large representation of baby boomers[8] in law firm partnerships. For law firms to thrive, much focus will need to be on effectively transitioning both the institutional knowledge and the relationships of these revered baby boomer partners and firm leaders.

Staff Attorney; Senior Staff Attorney

The work of staff attorneys is often less time-sensitive and typically not as rigorous or demanding. Staff attorneys usually fall into one of two categories: One group comprises attorneys who do not have the pedigree and/or experience to be on the equity partner path at the designated firm. The other group is made up of attorneys who have the same credentials as junior associates but who have elected the staff attorney path due to lifestyle reasons. For those in this latter group, if they elect to return to the junior associate path and have demonstrated their ability to do so, they should be able to transition back to the junior associate path as long as the business need exists. Staff attorneys content to remain on the staff attorney track or those who do not have the pedigree or experience to transition to another path, could then be promoted to be senior staff attorneys, a role that embodies work with similar characteristics to the staff attorney role but with more managerial responsibility.

---

8. There are 76 million baby boomers born between 1946 and 1964. "Meet the Generations," *Culture Coach International*, last modified 2010, http://www.culturecoach.biz/Generations/meetthegenerations.html.

Junior Associate or Junior Attorney; Senior Associate or Senior Attorney; Counsel

This path is for well-credentialed attorneys seeking to do interesting work but who do not want the extra responsibilities associated with partnership. At the outset, these lawyers may be junior associates or junior attorneys who are then promoted to senior associates or senior attorneys and eventually to counsel. A counsel-level lawyer would not have the pressure to generate clients that an attorney on a partnership track would have, but they are still valued lawyers committed to doing quality work with more predictable hours. Counsel-level lawyers may be assigned to less high-profile work, which is typically less erratic.

While for ease of reference, familiar terms like partner, counsel, staff attorney and the like, are used to describe the five sets of career paths outlined in the Olympic Rings concept, it is otherwise quite distinct from the prevailing Brass Ring model in the principal respects outlined here.

Even though the five career paths described above each reflect a promotion progression, that is not meant to suggest that everyone is automatically promoted. To the contrary, talent management decisions would be made at each promotion interval to determine if promotion is appropriate and if the attorney continues to meet the business needs of the firm or whether the attorney should no longer be employed at the firm.

Law firms have struggled with attracting, retaining, and promoting diverse talent, as we will explore more fully in Chapter 6. One of the reasons is because of the linear approach to talent development that has dominated the law firm culture. If law firms were to embrace career paths that cultivate Debbie's Olympic Rings of Talent, they would likely be able to attract and retain a more diverse representation of lawyers. What is critical to the Olympic Rings of Talent model and is evident in the Olympic Ring image is that there is fluidity in these paths. The circle image is important, as it shows continuity in progress as opposed to the traditional notion of lawyers going "off track" or being "on track." This addresses one of the entrenched problems with the traditional model: rigidity. Career paths are much less linear than the current law firm model dictates and a rigid approach is inconsistent with today's living. Nearly one-third of women lawyers leave the profession, independent of maternity leave, and women professionals who leave their professions do so for an average of three years.[9] The Olympic Rings give lawyers the flexibility to come in and out of the profession, consistent with the business and with their individual evolving needs.

In the Olympic logo, the rings are linked, which also applies in the law firm setting because of the inevitable overlap and need for lawyers to be able to cross over from one path to the other. Unlike the current system, under the Olympic Rings, one might begin on the staff attorney path and then elect to join the junior associate path. Assuming lawyers have the requisite credentials and experience to make the move and the business need exists, they would be able to comfortably transition from one path to another.

Valued alternatives to the equity partner path would likely be attractive to some of the attorneys from Generation Y (those born between 1980–2000[10]), who seek interesting, well-paid work but are not necessarily interested in the pursuit of partnership. If firms were to accept the ability of lawyers to cross over and move from one Olympic Ring to another, they would be able to retain more diverse talent who have traditionally not risen through the ranks at the same rates due to law firms' unforgiving and linear trajectory.

New legal models can be another vehicle for attorneys to create continuity in or reengage with their careers. Recall the story of the talented Bliss lawyer who lost his job during the economic downturn but was able to use the in-house engagement to find meaningful

---

9. Sylvia Ann Hewlett, Diana Forster, Laura Sherbin, Peggy Shiller & Karen Sumber, "Off-Ramps and On-Ramps Revisited," Center for Work-Life Policy (2010): 4, 21.
10. "Meet the Generations," *Culture Coach International*, last modified 2010, http://www.culturecoach.biz/Generations/meetthegenerations.html.

work that revitalized his career. His experience demonstrates how new legal models can also be used to get lawyers' careers back on track, providing an alternative path to progression.

It is clear that the Olympic Rings of Talent provide value to the individual lawyers in pursuit of alternatives to equity partner. But the question remains: What do the Olympic Rings of Talent have to do with value from the employer perspective? The short answer: everything. Much of the frustration around the billable hour is that it does not measure value. What the Olympic Rings of Talent do is provide another means to evaluate the service that each category of lawyer can provide. By providing five different ranges of career paths for lawyers, each with their own progression opportunities, the Olympic Rings further delineate the skill sets and contributions of different groupings of lawyers. In turn, this can help to better align the types of work, skills and seniority required for a particular representation with the lawyer or group of lawyers assigned to those tasks. It will also help to determine the appropriate fees that should be attached to both the tasks and the attorneys performing them.

Importantly, the Olympic Rings of Talent is governed by the business needs of law firms and the legal services' needs communicated by clients; this is what would dictate the roles and paths of law firm lawyers. With that in mind, creating valued alternative career paths would be a means to celebrate those who encompass a variety of promotion paths from which to choose, enabling attorneys and firms to find value throughout the Olympic Rings of Talent.

HOW DO WE VALUE A LAW FIRM?

The challenges of valuing a representation only by its number of billable hours and valuing a law firm associate principally by the hours or years logged are also echoed in the way the legal profession values a law firm. The prestige of a law firm has typically been determined based on a measure that, like the billable hour model, is in direct conflict with its clients. The gold standard for measuring a law firm's profitability is the profits per equity partner (PPP) created by the *American Lawyer* approximately 20 years ago.[11] The Am Law 100 or Am Law 200 ranks the profitability—and therefore the elite status of a law firm—based on the profits that each equity partner enjoys.

In fairness to the law firms featured, they did not create (and in many cases, do not espouse) this ranking. The *American Lawyer* created this vehicle, not dissimilar to the *U.S. News & World Report* rankings of colleges and law schools, which produce a significant ripple effect among the perceived status of the entities that attain its rankings. And while law firms that rank high on the Am Law 100 may feel a sense of pride, and may in fact be able to bill more per hour as they see their esteem increase, there are also negative impressions that these rankings leave. The risk with the Am Law rankings—and with the validation by earnings alone that it represents—is the possible negative impression of law firms in the minds of their clients.

Clients benefit from a firm that appears high up on the Am Law list when they are in "bet the company" litigation and have hired a prominent firm precisely for the purpose of bolstering their brand and position and intimidating opposing counsel. However, some clients are put off by firms that appear high on these lists. The feeling is one of remorse that they overpaid for a representation that is fattening the pockets of a few partners. Nothing erodes the trust that a client has in a law firm more than the feeling that they are being gouged for the exclusive purpose of personal gain. In corporate America, we consider profitability in terms of how the product or service is faring against its competitors. While this success inevitably affects the earnings of the executives of a particular company, it is not the focal point. However, when the compensation

---

11. "A Concise History of the Am Law 100," *American Lawyer*, last modified May 1, 2012, http://www.americanlawyer.com/id=1202543002248/A-Concise-History-of-The-Am-Law-100?slreturn=20140301101304.

packages of public company executives are made available, there is noteworthy and similar distaste when the earnings are disproportionate to the earnings of others.

There are other considerations for measuring the value of a law firm. What if law firms gave real credit to partners for contributions other than originating clients and billable hours? There are other significant contributions that partners can make like training and mentoring junior attorneys, developing the summer program, effectuating diversity and inclusion, working on recruiting and firm governing committees, chairing departments, and making other efforts as firm citizens that contribute to the successful operation of the firm. These efforts advance the partnership, develop the firm's attorneys, distinguish the firm's culture, and add value in ways other than landing a client. Until firms award credit (or notable credit) for these efforts, the result is to discourage time-pressured partners from contributing to the firm as a meaningful community.

CONCLUSION

And so the question may be asked: If the current law firm model does not support the value of the talent pool, or at least large sectors of the talent pool, and it does not support the value demands of many clients—who does it support? The inability to readily answer this question reflects an inherent problem in the profession today.

For real change to occur and to truly measure value, there needs to be a better design and alignment of what clients will pay for and what legal services providers and lawyers can provide. This reflects the need for change both in the employment model and at the individual lawyer level. The key will be determining how clients define value and at what level clients need services provided—and trying to mirror that with the talent pool's ability to produce at their maximum performance, efficiency and satisfaction.

3

PREDICTABILITY AND TRUST

JAMES W. CUMINALE, CHIEF LEGAL OFFICER, NIELSEN N.V.

The relationship of a company with its counsel, both inside and outside, represents a significant investment of time and money. This chapter addresses key returns every general counsel expects from those investments—predictability and trust.

First and foremost, we invest in and cultivate a relationship that makes the law firm and the lawyers working with us an extension of our company. The learning curve to understand any company is a long one. By concentrating our work with counsel over the long-term, they become familiar with our business, our culture, and our methods, which will enable them to exercise judgment aligned to ours and to deliver effective and efficient outcomes consistent with our expectations. Each engagement is a leap of faith by the company, and each successful outcome builds a level

Continued

JAMES W. CUMINALE, CHIEF LEGAL OFFICER, NIELSEN N.V. *CONTINUED*

of trust that allows us to delegate more and spread our reach across a greater span of issues and matters. On this aspect of the relationship, predictability and trust go hand in hand. The more we see judgment, approach, and outcome aligned with our expectations (predictability), the more we delegate (trust). And, of course, disconnects can be calamitous to the relationship.

This chapter also deals with a thorny issue of both predictability and trust—fees. While there is no easy solution to the challenge, every general counsel is under pressure to predict what is in many ways unpredictable—namely, the cost of reacting to the legal demands of the business. I know I value most the outside counsel who share that pressure with me by reducing the uncertainty of legal cost and getting to closure as efficiently as possible. This chapter addresses the various ways great counsel get there.

INTRODUCTION

We have talked about how the economic downturn of 2008 heightened the discussion regarding how law firms were providing value, whether there were feasible alternatives to the billable hour, and how growing client sophistication opened the door for a wider variety of legal service providers to take up disaggregated pieces of client representations. Integral to these changes in the profession are the concepts of predictability and trust.

PREDICTABILITY

Regardless of industry sector or geography, in-house legal departments are demanding more control of their legal budgets. General counsel are being pressured by their CEOs, who no longer allow in-house legal departments to exist without a real budget. As a consequence, general counsel have turned to their outside counsel with a plea for predictability.

As we have discussed, billable hours generally do not create or support predictability. They simply measure time logged, not projects completed or results achieved. Mitch Bompey, a Managing Director at Morgan Stanley, has experienced these circumstances many times over his career. In one recent incident, Mitch identified an important need in his group: a specific skill-set which would traditionally carry a heavy price tag if he chose a traditional law firm solution. Mitch understood that he had to marry his need for this specific skill-set with budgetary certainty and so he turned to the secondment option and fashioned a monthly fixed fee to create the predictability he needed.

You have heard that while many firms have explored alternative fees with their clients and such alternatives are underway, there is often a default back to the billable hour. Surprisingly, this default is prompted at times by the in-house lawyer. The reasons? We believe it is mostly due to convenience, history, and the general apprehension about change that is prevalent amongst many lawyers. Still, there are many that would argue that it is because billable hours is the method that works best. For in-house lawyers, billable hours remains the easiest way to compare lawyers when they are considering which firm to represent them. Relying upon the billable hour allows the law firm to remove almost all of the financial risk from the representation.

Additionally, in the interest of time, many fall back on the billable hour when there is not the opportunity to explore alternatives due to a time sensitive representation that arises. And of course there are ways to be creative while relying on the billable hour standard. Gene Park, Head of Alternatives Legal at AllianceBernstein, for example, has often found that using the billable hour in combination with reasonable caps on fees results in a high degree of budget certainty. Gene's creative approach in fashioning limitations on fees was particularly important after a reorganization at his firm left him with a reduction of in-house legal support at the same time that his group was experiencing an uptick in demand for legal services from the various businesses he oversees. Gene has been able to outline ways to reign in overall outside legal spend, but in a way that continues to fairly compensate his outside counsel, resulting in a sustainable partnership between the two.

The flat fee, where there is one predetermined price for a project or phase of a representation, is the fastest way to get clients to the predictability they need. Darren Pocsik, General Counsel of Financial and Risk at Thomson Reuters, was an early adopter of the flat fee as a way to ensure the comprehensive handling of major legal service needs. Early in his in-house legal career, Darren was faced with the likely sale of a major segment of his company's business. Rather than farming out various portions of the legal work to multiple firms, Darren decided to tap a single outside resource and negotiated a flat rate to handle virtually all of the necessary transactional work for the business until the completion of the sale. The result was the continuation of high quality legal services for the outgoing business but at a predictable and reasonable price for his company. Darren's decision to combine all of the work together under a single fee likely saved his company hundreds of thousands of dollars during this transitional period. It also had the important effects of allowing his in-house legal team to focus on the strategic needs of its continuing operations, while enabling the buyer to get an accurate idea of the resources it would take to support the commercial legal work of the purchased business.

Interestingly, when we developed our billing process at Bliss, we chose a flat weekly rate in an effort to be responsive to clients' repeated requests for predictability. Yet we inevitably get the question in response to providing our weekly flat rates, "So what does this work out to be per hour?" We find this curious because it is not as if our clients expect the lawyers employed by Bliss to punch the clock; they are professionals who are expected to work the roughly 50-hour professional in-house work week. Yet the hourly rate seems to be the easiest basis for comparison, and the standard by which the profession regularly turns to as a benchmark.

Even fee structures that some call alternative, like discounts or blended rates, are actually based on the billable hour, and thus they do not create the desired predictability. Take the blended rate, for example. In response to clients saying that they do not want to pay for a partner's time when they think an associate could do most of the work just as well, law firms often counter with a blended rate: where the partner may bill out at $500/hour and the associate at $300/hour, the firm puts both individuals on the representation and charges a blended rate of $400/hour for all the work performed. What this amounts to in the end is simply giving the in-house legal team a discount based on the same billable hour measure. Unfortunately, the corollary to this is that it gives the outside law firm an incentive to push the work down to the more junior lawyer who is less expensive and have the partner avoid working on the matter unless and until it is absolutely necessary. Additionally, the law firm lawyers may engender resentment for the client because the law firm cannot generate the full fee they desire for the work.

A real alternative fee not only creates predictability but also factors in a lawyer's expertise, efficiency, and ability to deliver results, as we have discussed. The classic example we provided is of the flat fee plus a bonus fee: The flat fee is based on a legal team's experience and anticipated efficiency whereas the bonus fee reflects the results—the "skin in the game." This combined flat and bonus fee approach can be very effective with certain types of work, e.g., mergers and acquisitions, litigation, etc. However, we recognize that it is not applicable in other circumstances, for example when a law firm drafts and negotiates subscription agreements, nondisclosure agreements, side letters, operating agreements, etc. The question then becomes: Why has the combined flat fee and bonus fee not become more popular in those practice areas where it meets a client's demand for predictability?

Some argue that the combined flat and bonus fee has not gained more momentum because it shifts the lack of predictability from the client to the law firm. While this argument reflects legitimate concerns, we think the law firm fear of unpredictability can be fairly addressed. Instead, we think the real obstacle to abandoning the billable hour and creating predictability, to put it simply, is a lack of trust. While a diminished trust is most readily apparent between client and law firm, in the legal profession it goes deeper. As we will explore, we see a lack of trust also manifesting among colleagues and legal service providers. We believe the very foundation of each of these relationships has become more tenuous, hindering lawyers' ability to perform at their maximum potential.

TRUST
Trust Between Law Firms and Clients

Trust between law firms and their clients is a thorny issue. In some cases, there is not only a diminishing trust among clients and law firms but also a palpable tension between them. Many misperceive the increasing distrust as coming solely from the client. This is shortsighted. In most cases, it is mutual, and what underlies much of the mistrust is fear. Law firms fear they will miscalculate what a representation will cost and they will lose out on well-deserved fees. Clients fear that law firms will overestimate an alternative fee to cover themselves in the event of an unanticipated circumstance, or worse, line their pockets at the client's expense. In both scenarios, it is fear that is preventing law firms and clients from developing an alternate means to value a representation.

As we have seen, clients have become more sophisticated since the economic downturn. They are no longer shy about asserting their needs. This often translates into a demand for discounts. Yet law firms have legitimate profitability concerns about adjusting their rates. They also have their own brands to protect. If a firm acquiesces to a client's request for a discount, this can lead to difficult staffing constraints. The discounted rate may necessitate that a matter be staffed by more junior lawyers. But the firm may be concerned that partner supervision is required in order to preserve the quality and consistency of the work product. Yet this will push down the actual realization rate, i.e., how much is earned on the engagement, costing the law firm money.

Clients may have reason for further concern when they request discounts. Natural economic forces would suggest that a firm may give more attention to clients who are paying higher rates (all other factors being equal), just as any for-profit enterprise would. Thus, the push–pull cycle between clients and law firms where clients recognize and use their leverage, and law firms that get squeezed on pricing in turn deliver less value, only further deteriorates the relationship. Some of the tension may stem from a lack of understanding of the full picture. From the in-house perspective, law firms often do not see the pressure that general counsel experience daily from their internal clients to control their budgets and manage the amount they spend on outside counsel. From the law firm perspective, in-house counsel may not recognize that applying pressure for discounts is not the same thing as devising a true alternative fee arrangement. Rather, it is just demanding the same service for less money. Additionally, when an in-house lawyer issues a request for proposals to multiple firms after a law firm has serviced its needs for years, it is hard for law firm lawyers not to feel diminished in the trusted advisor role they thought they held. This, in turn, risks reducing the law firm's loyalty to the client and the spiral of negativity continues.

Another tension arises when clients want to have a say in law firm staffing. A client's viewpoint may be inconsistent with the law firm's interest in developing its attorneys. Roy Shulman, Vice President and Chief Legal Officer, Operations and Systems, Prudential Financial, Inc. shared an example stemming from his efforts with law firms to channel the work to more junior attorneys.[1] Roy greatly appreciates when firms allow him to cultivate a relationship with a junior law firm lawyer, but he finds that firms often want senior associates or non-equity partners to assume responsibility for his matters. A law firm is in a tough spot under these circumstances. Legitimately, a firm needs to make sure the representation is handled responsibly and managed by someone with the appropriate level of experience and judgment. Additionally, from a professional development standpoint, senior associates and non-equity partners are at the stage of their career where they need to take ownership of more client relationships to show their potential for equity partner consideration. And, of course, the firm benefits from the fact that the senior associate and non-equity partner rates are higher. However, if the law firm approach is inconsistent with the client's wishes, staffing challenges will remain. Here, if the firm is resistant to Roy developing a close relationship with a junior lawyer, thereby showing him the firm's interest in building a legacy in talent and charging lower fees, Roy may be discouraged that the firm may not be truly committed to the company's future.

Restoring trust between clients and law firms is paramount to resume the discussion of how law firms can deliver the best value and provide clients with much needed predictability in fees. While the billable hour is still the predominant means of billing clients, there are important steps that law firm lawyers can take to rebuild trust. One is anticipating contingencies and ensuring that there are no surprises. Clients like to know what the conceivable outcomes may be at each stage of a representation, and a law firm lawyer who can lay that out will help ease the anxiety and unpredictability that typically attaches with billable hours. Stephen Gannon, General Counsel and Chief Legal Officer, Citizens Financial Group, Inc., makes the additional recommendation to law firm lawyers to

---

1. Based on remarks provided by Roy Shulman as a panelist at a Law & Reorder event entitled *What In-House Counsel Want*, New York, NY (March 11, 2014).

maintain contact and be willing to make mid-course corrections in a representation, where appropriate.[2] Steve finds it helpful for law firm lawyers to not only regularly check in but also solicit feedback from the client about how the representation is going, providing the opportunity to remedy certain courses of action that could be handled better. Steve advises law firms to not be afraid to project an image other than infallibility. We found Steve was not alone among in-house counsel in having these suggestions. Indeed, many in-house lawyers are seeking in their outside counsel a willingness to engage the client in decision-making and adjust recommendations when necessary.

Clients also emphasize the importance of law firm lawyers conveying to the client where they can contribute and when it is in the client's interest to seek alternative assistance. The credibility that law firm lawyers gain by knowing what to claim as their own and what to refer will serve law firm lawyers, as well as their clients, better in the long run. Ultimately, what constitutes a new vision of trust is an improved delivery of legal services where client and law firm interests are aligned and where law firms provide those services according to a profitable and sustainable model in a collaborative partnership with their clients and other legal service providers.

Trust Among Law Firm Colleagues

When we talk about the decaying trust in the legal profession, we usually only talk about it in terms of the law firm and client relationship. However, when we assess the layers of challenges facing the profession, we see that the lack of trust actually runs deeper. While the relationship between law firm and client may be the most obvious place where trust has dwindled, the deteriorating trust among colleagues in the law firm setting is also problematic.

---

2. Based on remarks provided by Stephen Gannon in a conversation with Deborah Epstein Henry, McLean, VA (May 14, 2014).

The legal profession has long thrived on the "eat what you kill" model, which basically states that lawyers are only as good as the last client they originated. Far from a team approach, this premise underscores that each person is in it for himself or herself. As a result, law firm lawyers lose opportunities to cross-market among practice areas and geographies. They also lose the ability to expand existing client relationships. This happens, at times, when law firm lawyers resist the sharing of credit when a lawyer who originates a client relationship shares partial credit (and earnings) with another colleague who has increased the amount of work the firm handles for the client. Ultimately, this resistance to share credit and work in teams will impede the firm's performance; colleagues will not feel a sense of ownership and commitment to the firm in the way that they would otherwise.

Law firm management's decision making, as well as its interaction with both associates and partners, can also impact trust. Some associates feel that the partners have not been as impacted by the economic downturn; their means of maintaining the status quo has been to lay off associates and cut other "costs." Some female and other diverse associates feel even more disenchanted, given their underrepresentation, particularly at the higher levels of seniority. Meanwhile, many in law firm management struggle to understand and inspire lawyers who comprise Generation Y—lawyers who, at times, are viewed as entitled and uncommitted.

For trust to be effectively established among law firm colleagues, it will require greater transparency, more effective communication, and a deeper investment in associate training. Patricia Gillette, a partner at Orrick, Herrington & Sutcliffe LLP had valuable insights to share on the subject of trust. She remarked: "The only way the trust dynamic changes is if law firms truly invest in their associates. That means hiring fewer attorneys out of law school, committing to meaningful and relevant training and development as attorneys and business developers, measuring their performance by something other than years out of law school and billable hours, and assuring these Gen Yers that there is some reward for their loyalty to the firm other than paying off law school debts."[3] Ultimately, we believe it will also require that colleagues are invested in each other's development and the overall success of the firm—and such investment is more valued than any individual lawyer's success.

Trust Among In-House Counsel

Historically, a challenge among in-house colleagues is the hierarchy, or lack thereof, within a company's legal department. Most in-house legal departments are flat organizations, giving talented in-house lawyers little opportunity to climb a corporate ladder. The increasingly coveted nature of in-house legal department jobs has kept many in-house lawyers loyal despite the lack of opportunities for ascendancy. While their loyalty to the company is generally intact, in-house legal departments have arguably become less hospitable as of late, largely due to the increases in work and changes in the in-house staffing model.

One staffing solution in-house legal departments have adopted is the secondment model we previously discussed—to bring in temporary high-caliber talent as a means to relieve the excess workload, reduce outside counsel spend, and avoid a headcount increase. Such alternative staffing has resulted in some of the permanent in-house lawyers being anxious about the security of their jobs. The concern is that perhaps the department will grow accustomed to the flexible staffing model and become inclined to transition more lawyers to temporary roles. These insecurities are exacerbated in some legal departments where staffing decisions are no longer entirely a legal department function—instead, some companies have their sourcing departments manage much of the staffing process.

Some in-house lawyers have devised successful ways to combat these challenges, empowering their team and in turn, strengthening

---

3. Based on correspondence by Patricia Gillette with Deborah Epstein Henry, San Francisco, CA (May 15, 2014).

the loyalty and trust among their colleagues. One lesson we learned from Karen Cochran, Assistant Chief Intellectual Property Counsel, DuPont, is the importance of frequent and candid communication.[4] By virtue of the training lawyers undergo to spot issues and to anticipate problems, some are more guarded and reluctant to be open for fear that it will expose them in some way. As a leader, Karen has learned that to be effective, she needs to be receptive and be willing to assume responsibility for her team. Through such outreach, she has seen that trust and loyalty are inspired by personal connection, one-on-one interaction, and honest communication.

When Kristine Wellman, Senior Vice President and Chief Counsel, Capital One, was the General Counsel of ING Direct USA, she found the most effective way to develop trust with her team was to empower them, each with their own budget.[5] By giving them ownership over their work and how it was executed, she found the team grew professionally—they did more challenging work in-house, they came in financially under budget in the year the program was implemented and they had fun and learned new skills in the process. Kristine attributes her team's strong performance to the increased accountability and trust that was engendered through her willingness to delegate and be confident that they would deliver. Another way to inspire trust is an approach shared by Sarah Francois-Poncet, Senior Vice President, Deputy Chief Legal Officer, Chanel.[6] She relayed that she inspires her team by ensuring that they retain some of the most interesting and challenging work—it is not automatically sent to outside counsel. The importance of ensuring that her in-house colleagues remain engaged in their work, reinforcing

---

4. Based on remarks provided by Karen Cochran in a conversation with Deborah Epstein Henry, Wilmington, DE (April 21, 2014).

5. Based on remarks provided by Kristine Wellman as a panelist at a conference, Wilmington, DE (March 25, 2011).

6. Based on remarks provided by Sarah Francois-Poncet as a panelist at a Law & Reorder event entitled *What In-House Counsel Want*, New York, NY (March 11, 2014).

their integral role in the business, is something that cannot be underestimated.

Trust Among Legal Service Providers

We have discussed how savvy clients are using a greater variety of legal service providers than ever before. Some will use secondment and virtual firms; outsourcing and insourcing companies; discovery firms; and global, national, regional, small, and solo law firms—many on the same representation. This panoply of options is far removed from the full-service law firm approach where the firm would provide all services related to the client's representation. Along with this change has come the necessity for competing legal service providers to foster trust with each other in an effort to deliver the best service and value to the client as an ensemble.

The imperative for competing legal service providers to collaborate has intensified since the economic downturn. This is partly due to the vast majority of in-house legal departments' success in consolidating and limiting their use of preferred law firms and other legal service providers. In so doing, the in-house legal departments have been able to increase their leverage to reduce their outside counsel spend. Given the smaller pool of outside vendors, some in-house legal departments have then taken the additional step of requiring that the select vendors work together.

Asking for trust among competitors may not be as difficult as it first appears when there are means to distinguish the value each legal service provider brings to the collaboration. A large law firm may be asked to team up with a much smaller firm that has a particular specialty. Since these firms would not otherwise necessarily be sharing clients, their fees are disparate, and their services are typically offered on a different scale; such an introduction would serve as a good referral source and is in fact customary. Moving from size to geography, a New York City law firm may be paired up with a law firm in Des Moines, for example, where they do not have a presence. Not only does this facilitate the necessities of appearing in court in Iowa, but also the combination of national and local counsel can provide a winning team when blended with the right chemistry.

When there is legitimate competition is when it gets more difficult. However, all legal service providers need to recognize that the clients are not only doing what is in their best interests by combining providers on a particular representation—they are doing what makes the most sense. A vendor who only does document review, for example, is not only more cost-effective for a client but also likely to be better at performing that piece of disaggregated work due to the volume of work of this sort that the vendor regularly handles. Those legal service providers who embrace these collaborations (rather than resist them) will ultimately deliver the best results to the client while being the most successful as businesses.

CONCLUSION

In order to create trust and regain the strength of the law firm and client relationship, it is helpful to start by providing transparency within the law firms and in-house legal departments themselves. In other words, trust must first be established from within the companies and the firms, and then there will be a better foundation to create it externally. Trust is the most desirable way to ensure an aligning of interests, an openness of dialogue, and an effective vehicle to create more predictability and anticipate and communicate unforeseen situations. Trust requires the legal profession to depart from its ossified ways and start different conversations, with the understanding that trust is a work in progress that will require ongoing adjustments.

4

FLEXIBILITY

JEAN MOLINO, GENERAL COUNSEL, MCKINSEY

As law students and lawyers, we have been trained to be circumspect—to anticipate risks and protect our clients from them. Some believe this is what our employers' value most about us if we work in-house, and why clients hire us if we work in law firms. But this misses a key part of our value proposition. Frankly, if we approach our advisory roles with risk mitigation solely in mind, our business partners will come to view us as obstructing the business rather than facilitating it. Instead, our clients, whether internal or external, want us to be creative and flexible problem solvers. I certainly look for this in my outside counsel, and it is an attribute we focus on in our legal department.

Creativity conjures up the notion of imaginative thought—a concept that is easy to grasp. But, flexibility comes in many stripes and can often be misunderstood. What flexibility means to me is an openness and responsiveness to situations as they are—to recognize that things are always changing, nothing is

Continued

fixed, and ideas and positions need to evolve in order to maximize impact and results. Flexibility is also about humility. As situations change, what is required is someone who can engage in give and take, who can recognize that not all approaches or solutions, even if they worked brilliantly in the past, may prove fitting as new information becomes available. We must be receptive to new ideas and changing direction as a matter of course. This is true not just for the advice we provide to our clients, but for how we work as legal professionals as well.

INTRODUCTION

Where lawyers are concerned, flexibility can mean many things. For years, flexibility has been viewed as an accommodation from the employer's perspective, with the associated connotation that lawyers who sought flexibility somehow embodied a lack of seriousness or commitment to the profession. When we look more closely, however, we see that flexibility is a means to create a win-win for both the employer and the lawyer. The flexibility that we will explore here is not about reduced commitment on the part of individual lawyers or increased accommodation on behalf of their employers. For employers, flexibility affords distinct advantages as a business driver when it is aligned with being agile and creating business efficiencies. For individual lawyers, flexibility can create opportunities to adjust career directions based on individual and employer needs.

FLEXIBILITY FOR EMPLOYERS

The events of the last decade, and in particular the impact of the economic downturn, foretold many of the evolutions in flexibility. In-house legal departments began to more affirmatively use the leverage that they held over outside counsel, demanding more flexibility in terms of how a particular matter was staffed and how they would be billed. Both in-house legal departments and outside law firms were forced into staff retraction, and even when the economic pressure began to lift, the immediate reaction on behalf of legal employers was not a rush to staff up to previous levels they had carried in the mid-2000's. Instead, employers sought flexibility in their hiring given the uncertainties that continued to loom. Rather than carry more personnel overhead, with the attendant risk of having to let individuals go again, employers sought to consider other options. These other options include getting more out of the staff that are already employed, bringing in contract lawyers, seconding lawyers from trusted law firms, and hiring secondment firms that provide lawyers when the engagement need arises.

Through the growth of the temporary talent pool, the use of contract lawyers has served firms and companies well. Contract lawyers are typically brought on through an outside firm or at an employer's own initiative to work on a project basis. The contract lawyer is distinguishable from a secondee because secondees typically are provided benefits and paid higher salaries and, in turn, secondment firms are usually able to attract a better credentialed and experienced lawyer. Companies will also, at times, second lawyers from their preferred law firm providers. The benefit of seconding a lawyer from a preferred law firm provider is that these lawyers have usually worked on that company's matters, so they come to the engagement both with institutional knowledge as well as a feel for the company's culture and the individuals with whom they will work.

There are also challenges with seconding lawyers from a law firm, including a reluctance of many firms to give up, for an extended period, experienced attorneys who actively manage multiple client matters. Additionally, the economic toll of lending out a senior associate at what is usually a discounted rate is often a significant cost. Firms are also reticent to have their clients borrow their star lawyers for fear of their top talent being poached. As a result, a company may be offered an attorney who does not have the appropriate skill set or requisite level of experience. During the downturn, many of the large law firms were loaning first year associates to their clients at no charge because they did not have enough work to keep these lawyers busy. The hope was that this would engender much good will for the law firm as well as help strengthen relationships with the client. These secondments had varying degrees of success. For those that were less successful, it was often attributable to the seconded lawyers' limited training and lack of experience.

The use of the secondment model, whether through law firms or secondment firms, grew in direct response to the increasing need for in-house legal departments to bring on high-caliber lawyers for temporary engagements without the "responsibility" for those lawyers long term. These responsibilities are considerable, as the employer assumes the employment risk as well as provides the employee salary, bonus, 401K, insurance, and other employee benefits. More specifically, by working with attorneys on a secondment basis, in-house legal departments gain both economic and risk-shifting benefits. The legal department avoids having to negotiate and pay severance or state unemployment insurance costs and also need not face the prospect that the lawyer may be the wrong fit for the team.

The secondment model, which originally evolved through the need to replace a lawyer on an *ad hoc* basis due to a medical or parental leave, has taken hold in the past decade as a more sophisticated and distinct market trend.[1] Today, the secondment need has

---

1. Jennifer Smith, "Companies Curb Use of Outside Law Firms—Staff Attorneys, Which Don't Bill by the Hour, Are Cheaper, Often More Efficient," The *Wall Street Journal*, last modified September 26, 2014, http://online.wsj.com/articles/companies

expanded well beyond these temporary leaves. High-caliber temporary lawyers who are staffed through secondment firms help companies through reorganizations and transitions, and they also help to build out legal departments to cover shifting workflows due to sudden employee departures, relocations, or changes in the market. Some companies use secondees to serve as subject matter experts in evolving or specified areas of law, e.g., Volker Rule, ERISA, etc. where it would be inefficient or too expensive to house a resident expert on a permanent basis. Companies also use secondment firms as cost-effective alternatives when they are simultaneously facing increased work yet pressure to reduce their outside counsel spend and work within hiring freezes.

One of the more interesting uses of secondment firms that we mentioned earlier is to provide companies with the luxury of "extended interviews." In today's market, the talent pool for experienced lawyers is quite strong, and we find that many unemployed lawyers have the substantive experience to do high-level work. With a bounty of qualified and talented lawyers, the criteria for hiring one lawyer over another becomes one of "fit." Is this lawyer going to fit in with a specific company's culture and be a strong contributor to the team? We have found that there is no better way to determine suitability than to actually afford clients the benefit of having attorneys start on a temporary basis. Once the client has ensured that an attorney is a good fit—after he or she has passed muster, so to speak—the company can then hire the lawyer directly.

In-house legal departments are not the only ones facing the issue of uncertainty in legal staffing. Law firms of every size are currently facing a similar judgment call about how they want to handle their staffing in terms of full-time or part-time, temporary or permanent,

-curb-use-of-outside-law-firms-1410735625; see also: Adele Nicholas, "Even as the economy recovers, law departments are still under pressure to do more with less," *Inside Counsel*, last modified September 27, 2013, http://www.insidecounsel .com/2013/09/27/even-as-the-economy-recovers-law-departments-are-s; Alex Newman, "Feeling the Squeeze—GCs Are Trying To Get as Much as They Can from Their External Advisers," *Legal Week*, last modified April 19, 2013.

as well as the varying degree of seniority and credentialing of their lawyers. The decision-making process that now includes a discussion of flexibility begins with the questions of who and how to hire. Do law firms want to attempt to solve all of their business needs with an internal stable of talent, or can their fluctuations in workflow be met most efficiently and cost effectively by tapping into new legal models and outsourcing some of their hiring needs as well? This is an issue we explored more fully in the Innovation discussion and is an operations decision that law firms should be seriously considering as they contemplate an evolving employment model. This question reflects not only the law firm's own economic health and stability and the reality of new client demands but also the startling advances made by technology over the last decade.

THE INTERPLAY BETWEEN TECHNOLOGY AND FLEXIBILITY

The fact that technology affords people the opportunity to work untraditionally seems like a commonplace assertion. Yet for the legal profession this shift has been slow to take root. Simply because we have the ability to avail ourselves of the great advantages of flexibility does not always mean we have done so or that there is a willingness to embrace the change that technology can offer to the profession.

Interestingly, one real push for legal service providers to incorporate the flexibility of new technologies came as a result of the tragic events of September 11. The chaos that resulted in the immediate aftermath of September 11 made it clear that organizations needed to have business continuity preparedness plans that allowed them to continue to deliver services in the face of large-scale crises, natural or otherwise. One critical facet of such a plan is to ameliorate workflow interruptions when physical access to the workplace may be impeded. This places a sharp focus on employers' steps to provide their employees the ability to work from home, or some other remote location, when necessary. In New York City, such plans put into place in 2001 positioned many companies and firms to be prepared in 2012 when Hurricane Sandy caused widespread and prolonged power outages in much of lower Manhattan.

The ability of lawyers at a firm to work seamlessly through a crisis is just one of the reasons why using the flexibility afforded by technology makes sense. Another is the ability to reduce real estate costs and to be able to pass those savings on to clients. Much of corporate America is being creative about reducing costs of real estate by having human resources and technology departments' work together to devise ways to reduce the actual need for real estate, which typically serves as the largest overhead drain. As we discussed in the Innovation chapter, traditional law firms are increasingly exploring such cost reductions by minimizing or substituting traditional office space and leveraging technology.

For some law firms, the reluctance to rethink their office space and, in turn, reduce real estate overhead, stems from a fear that such a move will tarnish their elite image. However, the firms that are leaders in reengineering office space are finding that the trend is gaining momentum and they are pleased to be ahead of the pack. For over a decade, Garry has seen the evolution in the mind of the client that getting top service no longer equates with where legal services are performed. Once more comfortable knowing that their lawyers were all stacked up in nice New York City offices, clients have increasingly realized that geography does not matter, nor does the kind of office in which a lawyer is working. What the client really wants is excellent and efficient delivery of legal services—if it means that they can pay less if such work is done remotely, then all the better. In fact, we can take this one step further and suggest that not only does geography generally not matter but also that clients are actually grateful not to pay for those swank, centrally located offices.

Clients have also learned that due to continuing advances in technology, there is usually no real need for lawyers to be sitting together in adjoining offices in order to be successful in working on a wide variety of client matters. And in fact, many law firm lawyers from the same firm who work together often do not see each other. This occurs both with law firm colleagues who have offices at the same address as well as lawyers who work from different geographies for the same firm.

Of course, in addition to the delivery of excellent legal services, clients are also concerned about their outside counsel's responsiveness and accessibility. While this question has not been specifically explored as it relates to lawyers working remotely on full-time schedules, the related concern that working reduced hours might negatively impact quality of work, responsiveness, and accessibility has been proved to be unfounded by the research. In one such study, clients were asked how they felt about working with outside counsel who worked reduced hours. The clients' response was simple: They had the same expectations of their outside counsel whether they worked full-time or reduced hours. The clients were satisfied as long as outside counsel maintained the same standard of excellence in their work product and they were responsive and accessible to the client.[2]

FLEXIBILITY FOR LAWYERS

Historically, the notion of flexibility as it relates to individuals has been raised within the context of work/life balance. Conversations about flexibility would often devolve into a win–lose proposition for the employer. The stigma around lawyers seeking flexibility is that these lawyers presumably lack commitment or want an accommodation that will inconvenience their company or firm. These notions of flexibility often still exist and we believe the concept of flexibility needs to be reframed. Instead, the focus needs to be

---

2.   Joan C. Williams, et al., "Project for Attorney Retention Corporate Counsel Project, Better on Balance?" *The Corporate Counsel Work/Life Report* (2003): 51.

on why and how incorporating more flexibility into every workplace is in the best interests collectively of clients, law firms, and lawyers. Indeed, flexibility is not just the future of work—it is its present as well.

It has been a long time since any business, legal or otherwise, has operated on a nine-to-five clock. When employers have lawyers who are used to working flexibly, it is typically much easier for them to take a call at midnight with a client or partner who is working in a different time zone across the world. This is just one example of how working flexibly is in fact being responsive to market demand. Additionally, while we have discussed many billable hour evils, one luxury of the billable hour is that the firm generates the same revenue from lawyers whenever and wherever they bill. While the billable hour is still the dominant means of billing clients, law firms can and should use the billable hour as an asset for their lawyers to gain more control of their day, all the while not impacting the economic model.

As an expert on work/life balance, Debbie encourages firms to capitalize on the benefits of flexibility. Yet many firms are afraid to do so for fear they will lose control of their workforce. This is shortsighted. Firms could increase their lawyers' productivity if they were more confident in their lawyers' ability to manage their time and if they provided some helpful parameters, including training on best practices, to make sure that business needs are met. When employers give lawyers flexibility in how they structure their day, these lawyers gain greater satisfaction in their lives, which feeds their efficiency, work quality, and loyalty.

Importantly, as we explore alternative scheduling, note that working flexibly is not the same as working reduced hours; many lawyers are willing to work full-time hours provided they have control in the ways in which they work. Working flexibly also does not always mean working from home. For example, Generation Y lawyers (those born between approximately 1980 and 2000), who represent the first generation that was raised on technology, view technology as a way of life. To not access the innovations of technology for these lawyers seems to them counter-intuitive and counter-productive. As a result of this exposure, many Gen Y lawyers have an expectation that flexibility will be part of their employers' work methodology. Greenberg Traurig LLP found this when it redesigned its Miami office space.[3] Its Gen Y lawyers told the partners that they did not want to be holed up in their offices all the time. In the office redesign, they suggested call-forwarding features and Starbucks-type cafe tables and congregating areas so that lawyers could work in teams collaboratively and from various locations. Even within an office space, therefore, Gen Y is looking for ways to work differently afforded by technology—it is about having a different mindset of how work should be performed and in turn, how the best work product will be produced.

This does not mean that flexibility is without its challenges. Debbie discovered this when she served as a consultant to the New York State Bar Association, during which she conducted a facilitation with partners from some of the large firms in New York who were in charge of associate issues. One of the partners' concerns was that Gen Y lawyers were asking for more mentoring and support—but they did not want to be in the office to receive it. These partners were trained and built bonds with their colleagues by spending nights and weekends reviewing documents together in the office or at the printer. Even though the partners who participated in the New York Bar facilitation were well-intentioned and wanted to encourage their Gen Y lawyers to express their needs, they were at the same time confused about how to provide feedback and a sense of community without actually being together.

Law firm partners are not alone in the flexibility predicament. Yahoo CEO Marissa Mayer triggered a national debate on the

---

3. "Greenberg Traurig's New Miami Office Focuses on the Future, City Core," gtlaw.com, last modified July 9, 2008, http://www.gtlaw.com/NewsEvents/Newsroom/PressReleases?find=107664.

subject when she announced a ban on working from home in 2013. As she relayed, while "people are more productive when they're alone . . . they're more collaborative and innovative when they're together. Some of the best ideas come from pulling two different ideas together."[4] The irony of a technology company issuing a statement of this sort was not lost on many. What the ensuing debate demonstrated, however, is that flexibility, like most things, requires a balance. There is no notable evidence that demonstrates that a conventional work week, with all employees on site is the magic that produces the best work at the best price. Yet, that does not diminish the value of face time and having colleagues work together during part of a traditional work week. Such in-person contact facilitates impromptu discussions and personal connections that help solidify trust as well as ingenuity in a working relationship. Thus, we believe the answer here is to both ensure that employees can gather together, share ideas organically, and build camaraderie, while giving employees the ability to work flexibly and individually to increase satisfaction and productivity. Taken together, these measures will contribute to the overall bottom line.

While pursuing flexibility has its challenges, the risks associated with being inflexible are not ones that the legal profession can afford. Take Suzie's experience for example. Suzie set out to become a large law firm partner. She worked for two top New York City law firms and, while she enjoyed the challenges presented in the actual work, she found the demands inconsistent with her family life. When the lifestyle became unsustainable, Suzie left the profession for five years. The flexible nature of a virtual law firm environment is what brought her back to practice. More than ten years later, Suzie has found a way to practice law at a high level on her own

---

4. Alexa Kleinman, "Marissa Mayer Finally Addressed Work from Home Ban," Huffington Post, last modified April 19, 2013, http://www.huffingtonpost.com/2013/04/19/marissa-mayer-work-from-home_n_3117352.html.

terms. She has been able to balance her time between her family, her work, and her community service, and she has found professional success and happiness as a result. Had a virtual law firm platform not been available to Suzie, she may never have returned to practice. Suzie is not alone among women. Thirty-one percent of women lawyers leave the profession, independent of maternity leave.[5] With women comprising 45–50 percent of enrolled law school classes for almost 30 years[6], the profession can no longer operate without maximizing the potential of all of its talent pool, whether these lawyers' paths are linear or not.

The issues around individual lawyer flexibility, however, are no longer specific to women. According to the National Association of Law Placement, in 2013, 30 percent of the lawyers who worked reduced hours were men.[7] Additionally, the Working Mother & Flex-Time Lawyers LLC Best Law Firms for Women annual survey found from the aggregated data of their 50 winning firms, that at each level of seniority, male lawyers were greater users of full-time flexibility than female lawyers.[8] Increased flexibility was certainly one of the prevailing reasons why Garry started his own law firm. And while Garry started his firm to achieve his own personal and professional goals, he has been gratified to see how flexibility has helped the 15 lawyers who work with him to achieve their personal and professional goals too.

---

5. Sylvia Ann Hewlett, Diana Forster, Laura Sherbin, Peggy Shiller & Karen Sumberg, "Off-Ramps and On-Ramps Revisited," Center for Work-Life Policy (2009): 8.
6. "First Year and Total J.D. Enrollment by Gender, 1947-2011," The American Bar Association, last modified 2012, http://www.americanbar.org /content/dam/ aba/administrative /legal education_and_admissions_to_the_bar /statistics /jd_ enrollment_1yr_total_gender.authcheckdam.pdf.
7. NALP, "Rate of Part-time Work Among Lawyers Drops for Third Year in 2013, Especially Among Women, But Most Working Part-time are Women," last modified February 27, 2014, http://www.nalp.org/part_time_pressrel_march2014.
8. "Best Law Firms for Women 2013, Executive Summary," Working Mother & Flex-Time Lawyers LLC, last modified 2013, http://www.flextimelawyers.com/ best/exsum13.pdf.

CONCLUSION

Individual lawyers who are flexible in their work methods are the ones who will ultimately succeed, given that the flexibility will enable them to meet the 24/7 demands of practice as well as their needs to balance the professional and personal demands on their time. As for clients, providing flexibility in staffing is what they want and what they need and therefore a rigid approach to staffing is not sustainable. For law firms, what this means is the need for further analysis to determine whether they will choose to mirror the more stratified staffing model of their clients for the analogous ebbs and flows of work. While law firms struggle with this challenge, we see that new legal models have found a way to align the marketplace and individual lawyers' desire for flexibility with an employer's need for profitability and efficiency. Perhaps the best way to capture this mutually beneficial flexibility solution is in the word agility. Indeed, the future of legal practice is ultimately about the agility of legal service providers to respond to and anticipate the needs of their clients as well as the agility of individual lawyers to respond to and anticipate the staffing needs of their employers.

5

TALENT DEVELOPMENT

DANIEL B. RODRIGUEZ, DEAN AND HAROLD WASHINGTON PROFESSOR, NORTHWESTERN UNIVERSITY SCHOOL OF LAW

The dynamics of contemporary legal practice require revisiting the relationship between law schools and law firms in the training of young lawyers. All that is certain is the uncertainty of exactly how the profession will change in the coming years. Predicting the nature and pace of change is always a risky enterprise. Yet, there is something especially vexing about the current climate in the legal profession, with structural impacts wrought by technology, globalization, and formidable economic forces ushering significant changes in the way in which young lawyers enter and thrive in these complex environments.

What are the law schools' roles in this period, which is somewhat opaquely labeled the "new normal"? Certainly, we will remain committed to the central imperative of providing law students with critical reasoning skills and the abilities to express

Continued

DANIEL B. RODRIGUEZ, DEAN AND HAROLD WASHINGTON PROFESSOR, NORTHWESTERN UNIVERSITY SCHOOL OF LAW *CONTINUED*

themselves in writing and orally. To put the point in finer terms, we should remain committed to a curriculum that helps our students to become articulate advocates and careful thinkers. Moreover, we should inculcate into these students the values of teamwork and leadership and, beyond this inculcation, develop in them the skills appropriate to a world in which collaboration is essential and in which lawyers will more often than not be part of, and eventually lead, teams of organized professionals. Finally, we should give opportunities for our students to use the important modern elements of big data and analytical methods, all to the advantage of their clients and causes. No doubt about it, there has been a sea change in the availability and compilation of information. Lawyers of the modern age will distinguish themselves through their abilities to develop heuristics, forge algorithms, and manage enormously complex bodies of information and data. These are skills that can and ought to be taught in law school.

The dichotomy between foundational, doctrinal knowledge and experiential learning is used too often in a confused and exaggerated way. Law schools are excoriated by lawyers for not doing enough to provide on-the-ground training; and law professors will frequently react defensively by insisting that their central role is teaching substance and not ensuring that their students are "practice ready." In reality, law schools can succeed in providing both fundamental knowledge and reasoning skills while also giving their students ample opportunities for turning this knowledge into action through clinics, simulations, and other experiential modalities. At their best, law schools build able lawyers through a marriage of doctrine and practice, substance and process. And, in our turbulent new normal, it is especially imperative for law schools to focus on both dimensions of these skills and on both layers of the legal curriculum.

Our times demand critical self-reflection, within both the bar and in the academy. Many law schools, including mine, are hard at work in constructing new forms of legal education and in refining our curricula to ensure that our students will be immediately capable to add value to law firms and their clients. With respect to pedagogical techniques, innovations such as "flipped classrooms" and the use of case studies will help our students become better lawyers faster. And, with respect to specific curricular foci, developing courses and seminars that expose students to new areas of law and, importantly, to the intersections among law, business, and technology will enhance their abilities and benefit their employers.

We are in an exciting era in both the practice of law and the education of law students. Never has it been more important for legal educators to join with professionals in the legal training space, both within and outside law firms, in order to forge novel initiatives and promote good ideas. In this book, the reader will see examples of these innovations come to life.

INTRODUCTION

Would-be lawyers are getting the message loud and clear that the path to becoming a successful lawyer is much less certain than even ten years ago, and the risks of unemployment and significant debt following law school graduation are unfortunate realities. Given the uncertainty of the legal job market, law school applications are steadily declining. As for those graduating law students entering the profession, the increasing concern is: Who will absorb the cost and responsibility for training new lawyers? We focus in this chapter on training and developing lawyers—as we believe there is a crisis in talent management and that training and development is both the link and the key to increased law school applicant admission and lawyer employment.

Let's start with the numbers. According to the Law School Admissions Council, the number of applicants to law school in 2013 fell below 60,000 for the first time since 1983.[1] By contrast, the high-water mark for applicants in 2004 showed over 100,000 individuals applying to ABA-accredited schools.[2] Of the 2013 applicants, fewer than 40,000 matriculated as full-time or part-time students in a J.D. program, the lowest since 1977.[3] What makes these figures even more startling is that the last time the number of enrolled students dipped so low, there were 24 fewer law schools. In other words, universities may have built their field of dreams, but many of the players have stopped showing up.

WHY IS THE PROFESSION WELCOMING FEWER LAW STUDENTS AND LAWYERS?

Why has the dip in law school applications and matriculation dropped so dramatically? Several factors are contributing to this spiral of decline. We can begin with changes in the profession that dictate the need for fewer lawyers in the first place, or at least fewer lawyers to occupy some of the more well-known rungs on the talent ladder.[4] While there may not be fewer jobs per se, there are fewer entry-level jobs for the lawyers at the highest

---

1. "Three-Year Applicant Volume Graph," Law School Admissions Council, last modified 2014, http://www.lsac.org/lsacresources/data/ethnic-gender-matriculants; see also: Staci Zaretsky, "Law School Applications Plummet" *The Law*, last modified August 20, 2013, http://abovethelaw.com/2013/08/law-school-applications-continue-to-tumble/.
2. "End of Year Summary: ABA Applications, Applications, Admissions, Enrollment, LSATs, CAS," Law School Admissions Council, last modified 2013, http://www.lsac.org/lsacresources/data/lsac-volume-summary.
3. Mark Hansen, "Law School Enrollment Down 11 Percent this Year over Last Year, 24 Percent over 3 Years, Data Shows," *ABA Journal*, last modified December 17, 2013, http://www.abajournal.com/news/article/law_school_enrollment_down_11_percent_this_year_over_last_year_data_shows/?utm_source=maestro&utm_medium=email&utm_campaign=daily_email.
4. See generally Richard Susskind, *The End of Lawyers?: Rethinking the Nature of Legal Services* (New York: Oxford University Press, 2010).

levels of practice, where the elite law schools have traditionally propelled their graduates. As the stratification of legal service providers continues, the number of jobs available arranges itself accordingly.

Law firms that once employed large classes of incoming associates started shrinking the size of those classes considerably beginning with the economic downturn of 2008. As this retraction continues, it has had ripple effects throughout the law school continuum. A smaller class of incoming associates means more competition among the most elite law school students. As the top jobs become harder to get, students that graduate from second-tier schools in turn have even fewer chances of landing jobs that can provide security. Indeed, the prospect of finding a secure job with a viable career path and an income that allows for the steady pay-off of student debt and an acceptable standard of living is becoming more remote.

And, make no mistake, security is important. How do prospective lawyers envision future careers when fewer legal employers are willing to commit to hiring them or only on a temporary basis? How do these lawyers buy a house, start a family—in short, how do they do all of the things that those established in the field have done when these new lawyers are working in an increasingly lean and precarious talent model?

Law school is an investment. To make this investment, which at private law schools recently topped $40,000 a year in tuition and is nearing $25,000 a year at public schools, 90 percent of law students finance their education by taking on debt.[5] The average debt of private law school graduates nears $125,000; it hovers just

---

5. Debra Cassens Weiss "Tuition and Fees at Private Law Schools Break $40K Mark, on Average" *ABA Journal*, last modified August 20, 2012, http://www.abajournal.com/news/article/average_tuition_at_private_law_schools_breaks_40k_mark/; see also: Equal Justice Works, "Law Schol Student Debt is Just the Tip of the Iceberg." *U.S. News*, modified on February 1, 2012, http://www.usnews.com/education/blogs/student-loan-ranger/2012/02/01/law-school-student-debt-is-just-tip-of-the-iceberg.

over $75,000 for public law school graduates.[6] This causes pro
spective law students to have legitimate doubts as they look down
their intended career paths.

As the next generation of lawyers receives the clear message that
there are going to be fewer opportunities in the field, and that there
is a real and significant risk that they will graduate with debt they
cannot repay, the concern is that the caliber of the applicant pool
will inevitably shrink. This challenge stems from the thought that
fewer talented students will seek law school as a career path for
fear they will not get a proper return on their investment. In turn,
law schools will need to admit less qualified applicants to fill their
classes. What all of this leads to is a crisis in talent development of
the legal profession where many of the key stakeholders, including
law school administrators, law firm partners, and in-house lawyers,
are pointing the finger somewhere else. We think, however, that
within these prickly problems lie some potential solutions.

SHRINKING INCOMING ASSOCIATE CLASSES

We have previously explored the increased stratification of legal
service providers as well as new and emerging legal service models.
What most of the new legal service models have in common is that
historically they have relied on larger law firms to train the legal
talent pool. In essence, law firms have trained entry-level associates and have shared this cost with their clients through fees billed
to in-house legal departments. This is as important to incoming
associates who seek employment at a larger firm long-term as it is
to those who are intent on pursuing a more flexible path such as
a secondment—every attorney must receive appropriate training.
It is not a step that can be skipped.

---

6. Debra Cassens Weiss "Average Debt of Private Law School Grads is $125K;
It's Highest at These Five Schools," *ABA Journal*, last modified March 28, 2012,
http://www.abajournal.com/news/article/average_debt_load_of_private_law_grads
_is_125k_these_five_schools_lead_to_m/.

However, increasingly clients have begun pushing back. No longer will they allow outside counsel to staff their matters with junior associates who are largely inexperienced and inefficient, yet still quite expensive. Or, if clients do allow junior lawyer staffing, then they require that these junior lawyers are billed out at a significant discount to reflect the actual value and contribution that a first or second year associate can realistically provide. Clients have also gotten savvier about the kinds of lawyers assigned to their work. They may not feel that they need graduates of the most elite schools staffed on their more routinized matters, depending upon how demanding or sophisticated they see the work. For example, clients may insist that graduates with varying credentials and billing rates handle the work that mirrors their capacity and require that the fees are commensurate with the matters to which they are assigned. What this reflects is that the training model has changed—there has been a retrenchment—and we can only anticipate that this market trend will continue. Now law firms have to make some tough decisions: Can they afford to absorb the training cost of junior lawyers without the same subsidy from clients? Are they going to bring in fewer attorneys? Can they ask more of the law schools?

THE ROLE OF TODAY'S LAW SCHOOL

Increasingly, the legal community has turned to law schools and proclaimed it unacceptable to produce graduates with upwards of $125,000 in loans without—according to some—the practical skills to practice law. Many law firm partners argue that it is no longer enough for law schools to produce graduating law students who merely know how to "think like a lawyer" as the expression goes; now law firms are increasingly looking for practice-ready graduates.

The question arises as to how law schools might navigate this demand, and if it is appropriate to expect them to do so. Top tier law schools are very clear that they do not want to devolve into trade schools. While scores of law schools have added more practical, hands-on classes, for many this is not enough—they argue that an overhaul of the entire legal education system is in order. Along these lines, in 2012 an American Bar Association (ABA) Task Force on the Future of Legal Education (Task Force) was created with the purpose of examining the legal landscape and making suggestions about how the ABA, law schools, and other legal organizations can address the issues of the cost and delivery of legal education.

In January 2014, the Task Force released its final report (the Report), calling on law schools, bar associations, regulators, and others to redesign the financial model now prevalent in law schools, revise the system that accredits law schools to permit more experimentation and innovation, and expand opportunities for the delivery of legal services. The Report attributes the catalyst for its recommendations to be the "pressure because of the price many students pay for their education, the large amount of student debt, consecutive years of sharply falling applications, and dramatic changes, possibly structural, in the market for jobs available to law graduates."[7]

While the Report has not yet been approved by the House of Delegates or the Board of Governors of the ABA, its key recommendations reflect the direction of the conversation and debate that is currently underway in the legal community.

The Report recommended:

1. The ABA should create a body to examine in detail the cost and funding of legal education.
2. The ABA should institutionalize an assessment and improvement of the law school system.
3. The ABA should establish a mechanism to institutionalize the process of assessing and improving the legal education system.

---

7. ABA Task Force on the Future of Legal Education, "Report and Recommendations American Bar Association Task Force on the Future of Legal Education," American Bar Association, last modified January 23, 2014, http://www.americanbar .org/content/dam/aba/administrative/professional_responsibility/report_and_ recommendations_of_aba_task_force.authcheckdam.pdf.

4. The ABA Section of Legal Education and Admissions to the Bar, which accredits law schools, should loosen or eliminate the accreditation requirements that raise the cost of a legal education without corresponding increases in education quality.

5. Other legal regulatory authorities should research ways to lower education requirements for admission, and should consider proposals that would allow select legal services to be provided by people without JDs.[8]

It remains to be seen which of these recommendations, if any, will be adopted and in what form. But the in-depth self-exploration of the crisis by American lawyers itself reveals a deep desire to take control of legal education and redirect its future. Some of the debates that will persist into the future include how to continue to attract law students to more affordable legal education, how to enable law students and law schools to thrive while producing practice-ready graduates, whether to invite non-lawyers into the legal service arena, whether relaxing the requirements for law school entry will negatively impact the quality of graduating law students, and how lawyers can become more responsive to the changing demands of clients and the global legal marketplace.

CHANGING THE LEGAL TRAINING MODEL

It is not acceptable for those of us who are not legal educators to wash our hands of the challenges and simply be glad that we are not a law school dean who is responsible for these students or a recent law school graduate trying to pay off enormous student loans and find a job practicing law. If we care about the future of the legal

---

8. Mark Hansen, "ABA Task Force Calls for Sweeping Changes in Legal Education System," *ABA Journal*, last modified January 24, 2014, http://www.abajournal.com/news/article/aba_task_force_calls_for_sweeping_changes_in_legal_education_system/.

profession, we should all be concerned about how to continue to attract the best and the brightest and how to train our future leaders.

As Debbie has closely followed the debate about what she calls "junior lawyer fallout" and the crisis around who will absorb the cost and responsibility of training junior lawyers,[9] she has come up with some ideas of her own about how to address this conundrum.[10] Her best recommendation is, in a word: outsourcing.

We have discussed the growing use of outsourcing as a means to deliver legal services. In-house legal departments regularly out-source the legal support they need in seeking outside counsel and using other legal vendors to support the discovery process and otherwise. Generally, though, we have not explored the notion of outsourcing practical skills training for lawyers. While the legal profession is in essence a highly traditional profession, there are already powerful examples of legal training outsourcing such as the BARBRI review course. This six week class, designed to help recent law school graduates pass the bar exam, is taken by a critical mass of aspiring attorneys. BARBRI attests that taking its bar review class increases passing percentage rates by over 12 percent, with some participating law schools reporting a 20 percent increase in passing percentage rates.[11] Bar review courses have become such an accepted truth that when an incoming associate gets a job at a law firm, that firm will often pay the student's BARBRI (or other respected bar review class) fees, just as if it were paying for a new hire's moving expenses.

---

9. Deborah Epstein Henry, *Law & Reorder: Legal Industry Solutions for Restructure, Retention, Promotion & Work/Life Balance* (Chicago: American Bar Association, 2010): 30.
10. See generally: Deborah Epstein Henry, "Combating Junior Lawyer Fallout—Part I," Law360, last modified March 25, 2011, http://www.lawandreorder.com/press/press21.pdf and Deborah Epstein Henry, "Combating Junior Lawyer Fallout—Part II," Law360, last modified April 1, 2011, http://www.lawandreorder.com/press/press23.pdf.
11. BARBRI, "Improving Bar Exam Passage Rates," BARBRI.com, last modified summer 2012, http://www.barbri.com/lawSchools/barPassage.html.

Rather than rely on law firms or law schools to handle bar review preparation, the legal profession has accepted the value of outsourcing by well-respected bar review companies in a critically important stage of an individual's transition from law student to lawyer. Another compelling example of outsourcing that has become accepted in the legal profession training arena is the use of the National Institute for Trial Advocacy (NITA) to train trial lawyers.

NITA trains litigators in the skill sets that are integral to becoming a successful trial lawyer, such as how to depose a witness, how to effectively handle and use exhibits, and how to cross-examine a witness at trial. Many in the legal profession have no difficulty in assessing the value of this form of outsourcing. Having every law firm in the country train its own litigators on these critical skills is too cumbersome, too expensive, and less effective. Instead, high level litigators from top law firms all over the country go to off-site locations to participate in intensive NITA courses. If learning the techniques of becoming a great trial lawyer can be supplemented by an outsourced organization such as NITA, why, by extension, can we not accept the outsourcing of training in the required core competencies to develop a practice-ready lawyer?

Rather than have each law firm continue to incur the costs of training its incoming attorneys, what if that cost were shared and all law firms paid a significantly reduced fee to send their first and second years to periodic core competency training? Not dissimilar to the core competency training models devised at certain firms, the first and second year curriculum could include general skills that all lawyers should have, e.g., written communication, oral communication, professional ethics, etc. Additionally, there would be core competency skills taught for each major practice area and lawyers would be divided into practice area groups accordingly, e.g., first and second year litigators would be taught the foundations of the discovery process, drafting motions, spotting issues, etc. Law firms could then supplement the outsourced core competency training of their lawyers to the particular style of that firm. Such expense that a firm may elect to incur to tailor the training would be dramatically reduced, given the foundation that their lawyers would glean through the outsourced model.

In March 2013, in a plenary session to the ABA Bar Leadership Institute, Debbie made this recommendation and suggested that the state bar associations assume the role of the trusted outsourcing core competency body to train junior lawyers. She suggested that this core competency training could be subsidized by the employers of recent law graduates who would be paying a fraction of the training costs that they would otherwise incur. This would address another challenge to the profession that we will address in a subsequent chapter—the relevancy and future role of bar associations. Of course, this function could also be outsourced to other non-profit and for-profit enterprises as well.

In contemplating who would train new lawyers the skills to become practice-ready, the profession could turn to many of the retiring baby boomer lawyers. Incidentally, this would help these baby boomers too, as many are struggling with their own questions about how to effectively transition into retirement. Unlike most law professors who have not had much, if any, exposure to traditional practice, retiring practitioners have a lifetime worth of skills to effectively impart to developing lawyers. Ideally, these baby boomers would provide this service to the bar on a *pro bono* basis, and perhaps the hours devoted would serve as continuing legal education credit that these practitioners would otherwise need to fulfill.

Much of the discussion around junior lawyer training has focused on law school reform. While it is clear that law schools should continue to reevaluate their curriculum and role, to expect true innovation and a revamping from law schools may ultimately prove very challenging. When contemplating law school reform and rethinking legal education, there are many considerations and nuances that are in need of exploration. Should law schools shrink the curriculum and shift from three years to two? Should the third year become a guided internship, more in line with the Canadian apprenticeship model or the medical profession model? Should the law school tenure track be reformed or eliminated? These are among the issues, in addition to those raised by the Report, which will need to be further debated and considered. In the meantime, the training of junior lawyers continues to deteriorate on a daily basis. To address this issue, we need to move beyond the conversation of what law schools will do, what clients are willing to pay for and what individual law firms can no longer afford. Instead, we need to think more creatively about how to pool resources and use the outsourcing trends in today's marketplace to invest in the future generation of lawyers.

CONCLUSION

The innovations in new and traditional legal models have come from a combination of prior failings in traditional models and the shifting demands for legal services. These factors have not similarly served as compelling drivers for innovation and change in talent development. As the current and future legal service providers evolve and begin to look very different, it is unrealistic to expect that the training modules will be able to stay the same. Thus, innovation must occur at every layer and level from legal education to junior lawyer training to the sophisticated practice of law. While the Task Force recommendations are crucial considerations for legal education reform, junior lawyer training must receive the same in-depth analysis in order to ensure the successful continuum of talent development.

6
DIVERSITY AND INCLUSION

THOMAS L. SAGER, PARTNER, BALLARD SPAHR LLP; FORMER SENIOR VICE PRESIDENT AND GENERAL COUNSEL, DUPONT

Organizations throughout the United States, both corporate legal departments and law firms alike, are facing intense competitive pressure. To survive and thrive, companies and firms must continue to embrace and advance a culture that values diversity and inclusion. For those of us who have held positions of prominence, it is incumbent  upon us to use our platform to set the right tone. We must have the vision and resolve to foster a culture that identifies and regularly engages those diverse professionals at all levels of the organization. And then we must create truly meaningful opportunities for them to help us solve our most pressing business problems and challenges. It is only through this commitment to diversity and inclusion that organizations will successfully renew themselves and secure their future.

INTRODUCTION

Throughout this book, we have seen that the success and evolution of the legal marketplace, along with the development of new legal models and the innovation of traditional legal models, hinges on how effectively the talent pool meets the changing demands of the profession. In order to maximize the effect and impact of the talent pool, we must ensure that diversity and inclusion (D&I) are valued and integral to the delivery of legal services at each step of the process.

At the outset, we want to be clear that we believe the goal of a truly diverse and inclusive profession is not a shift in the balance of power for its own sake. If we get to the point where women and people of color refer business exclusively to other women and people of color, this is not progress to celebrate. The victory in D&I lies in providing opportunity, variety, and choice. Increased D&I throughout law firms and other legal service providers, in-house counsel teams, and non-legal professionals is necessary to reflect the diverse customer base of clients and employees that presently exists and will continue into the future.

As we explore the subject of D&I, there are a couple of important ground rules to establish. The first is that we want to be careful about stereotyping in general, or painting the issues with too broad a brush. An Asian woman and an African American man in the legal profession, for example, do not have the same experiences—neither do two Asian women or two African American men, for that matter. To eliminate these complexities in favor of an overarching concept of D&I would be a mistake. The other ground rule we would like to acknowledge is that when we talk about D&I, the "I" is just as much a crucial component as the "D." In other words, we are not seeking to exclude anyone from the discussion. D&I is an acknowledgment of the effectiveness that a diverse environment provides for employers, employees, and clients. The goal is to create more readily available opportunities in terms of roles and models for all lawyers, and to determine the most effective way to truly achieve D&I in a changing profession.

WHERE ARE WE NOW?

To figure out how D&I might evolve in a profession of shifting models and markets, we first need to ascertain where we are now in terms of overall legal employment and elevated status, such as law firm partnership. The National Association for Law Placement (NALP) tracks minority attorneys including those whose race or ethnicity is black, Hispanic, American Indian/Alaskan Native, Asian, Native Hawaiian, or other Pacific Islander, and those of multi-racial heritage. Also included in the NALP diversity statistics are women, lawyers with disabilities, and lesbian, gay, bisexual, and transgender (LGBT) lawyers, each category of which is separately tracked. Minority women are also separately tracked as a category.

The results are not pretty. According to NALP, while minorities account for little more than 20 percent of all associates and staff attorneys, at the partner level, that number falls to about seven percent. The percentage of partners who are minority women dwindles even further to about two percent.[1] This increased drop for minority women is attributable to a "double bind" that minority women face where they confront additional obstacles in being both minorities and women.[2]

While the NALP data applies to law firms, the statistics for in-house counsel are not appreciably better. The Minority Corporate Counsel Association (MCCA) releases its annual survey results of Fortune 1,000 women and minority general counsel. Its 2013 survey report shows 19 percent of women held the position of chief legal officer. Among the Fortune 500, minority women comprised four percent of the 21 percent women general counsel, two percent of

---

1. The National Association for Law Placement. "Women and Minorities at Law Firms by Race and Ethnicity—An Update," NALP Bulletin, last modified February 2014, http://www.nalp.org/0214research (figures based on over a thousand law offices and firms totaling more than 110,000 lawyers).
2. See generally Kimberle Crenshaw "Intersectionality: The Double Bind of Race and Gender" Perspectives, last modified Spring 2004, http://www.americanbar.org/content/dam/aba/publishing/perspectives_magazine/women_perspectives_Spring2004CrenshawPSP.authcheckdam.pdf.

whom were African American women, one percent Hispanic women, and less than one percent Asian American women. Of the 17 percent women general counsel in the Fortune 501–1,000, one percent were minority women. Total, there are seven percent minority general counsel in the top 1,000 companies.[3] Joseph K. West, MCCA President and CEO, notes that "the number of women attorneys leading the legal departments of these top-grossing companies continues to increase. These numbers show progress, however slowly, in the diversity and inclusion within the legal profession, but all legal leaders must dedicate themselves to offering more women within their departments increased opportunities for mentoring, development and career growth for there to be parity with male legal leaders."[4]

SLOW PROGRESS AMONG WOMEN AND PEOPLE OF COLOR

When we reflect on the slow progress among women and people of color, we note that recruiting, retention, and promotion continue to be the key challenges impacting diversity efforts. Importantly, though, not all minorities struggle equally with these prevailing challenges. For example, there is generally not an issue with white women and recruiting—the issues for white women are largely about retention and promotion. LGBT lawyers also may not face the same challenges with respect to recruiting, which is largely due to the fact that their diversity is often not readily apparent—a lesbian lawyer may be able to downplay her sexual identity[5] in a

---

3. "The Continuing Climb: Diverse GCs Power Up, MCCA's 14th Annual General Counsel Survey," Diversity & the Bar, last modified Sept./Oct. 2013, http://content .yudu.com/A2cmbh/DivTheBarSepOct2013/resources/1.htm.
4. "MCAA Survey: Women General Counsel at Fortune 1000 Companies Increase," Minority Corporate Counsel Association, last modified September 16, 2013, http://www.mcca.com/index.cfm?fuseaction=Feature.showFeature&featureID=450.
5. "Covering" describes the process of downplaying aspects of one's identity. See generally Kenji Yoshino, *Covering: The Hidden Assault on our Civil Rights* (New York: Random House, 2006).

way that an African American lawyer more often cannot conceal his or her ethnicity.

When looking for explanations behind the sluggish D&I efforts, it is important to look at all of the constituents involved. While the focus on D&I should legitimately be on historically disadvantaged groups, progress cannot be made without making allies of those in power, often white men. A Catalyst study which focused on engaging men as champions of women found that only when men truly believed that there was a problem with the status quo would they begin to lobby and support efforts to increase D&I. The more a man was aware of gender-based biases, the more likely that man was to believe in the importance of gender equality measures.[6] The Catalyst study found that simple awareness of gender bias was not enough, however, as there exist multiple obstacles that prevent men from supporting women. Apathy, fear, and real or perceived ignorance were the three largest barriers, with fear being cited by 74 percent of male interviewees.[7] This fear could play out in a number of ways. Some men fear that equality for women would come at a harmful cost to men.[8] For example, if there are 15 seats on the Executive Committee of a firm and a male member advocates for a woman to be brought on to the Committee, the other men may worry they will lose their coveted spot. Men also feared criticism, both from women who saw all men as part of the problem and from male colleagues whose disapproval would result in perceived loss of masculinity.[9] Other men may fear that attempts to support women colleagues would be misconstrued as romantic interest, or that a male attempting to enact change would be an ineffective champion of a women's cause.[10] Many of these fears, including a fear of providing real feedback in an evaluation, may result in

---

6. Jeanine Prime & Corinne A. Moss-Racusin, "Engaging Men in Gender Initiatives: What Change Agents Need to Know," *Catalyst*, 2009: 5.
7. Ibid. at 14.
8. Ibid.
9. Ibid. at 15.
10. Ibid. at 16.

creating a real chilling effect in the workplace. Addressing these fears, whether seemingly legitimate or not, will become central to the success of any D&I initiative.

Beyond addressing fears, it is important that white men are active participants in the D&I efforts so they become invested in the issues and the vision of their organizations. One way to achieve that is by inviting white men to play leadership roles in diversity committees. This provides white men with the opportunity to not only develop a greater understanding of the complexities of the D&I issues but also became more deeply committed to address them. Having white male colleagues become ambassadors to the D&I cause is critical to bridging communication and bringing unity to the D&I issues in organizations.

While most D&I initiatives tackle a range of subjects, one thing they all seem to have as a common focus, as it impacts all minority groups, is a paucity of representation at the top. This cannot be blamed merely on inadequate recruiting. In the case of white women, for example, there is no shortage of such lawyers—at least at the start. For nearly 30 years, female law school students have comprised 40– to 50 percent of the total enrollment in J.D. programs.[11] However, representation of women equity partners at law firms hovers at 17 percent.[12] Some have attributed women's lack of critical mass at the equity partner level to be due to a pipeline problem. However, the issue cannot be conveniently explained this way, as there has been no shortage of women entering the profession. Something else is going on—the challenges for white women

---

11. "First Year and Total J.D. Enrollment by Gender, 1947–2011," The American Bar Association, last modified 2012, http://www.americanbar.org/content/dam/aba/administrative/legal_education_and_admissions_to_the_bar/statistics/jd_enrollment_1yr_total_gender.authcheckdam.pdf.
12. "Report of the Eighth Annual NAWL National Survey on Retention and Promotion of Women in Law Firms," National Association of Women Lawyers, last modified February 2014, http://www.nawlfoundation.org/pav/docs/surveys/Eighth_Annual_NAWL_Survey-Final.pdf.

revolve around retention and promotion, while with women of color, recruiting challenges continue as well.

There are many negative results of the minimal representation of women and people of color at the top. One significant impact that is often overlooked is the notion of "covering." This is the reluctance of diverse talent to bring their authentic selves to work which in turn prevents them from producing at their maximum capacity.[13] When diverse talent is underrepresented, especially at the leadership levels, the resulting missed opportunities for the business, in addition to the individuals, is significant. Thus, employers need to recognize that building an inclusive work environment will enable individual employees to thrive and, in turn, improve the bottom line.

TYPES OF BIASES

Many workplaces have yet to build an inclusive environment and are in the initial stages of confronting the lingering biases that remain. The term "unconscious bias" is an umbrella term for the unconscious attribution by an individual of particular qualities to a member of a certain group. Often these perceptions, attitudes, and stereotypes will emanate from individuals without their intention or awareness. One way this plays out in the workplace is when employers become partial to white men over minorities and women with respect to job offers, promotions, and raises. The unconscious bias can be especially harmful when individuals are placed in the role of evaluating others or they are otherwise in a leading capacity. Regardless of their active efforts to be fair and impartial, unconscious bias is often an unrecognized prejudice—and as a Catalyst study showed, one needs to be aware of prejudices before they can be countered.[14]

---

13. See generally: Kenji Yoshino, *Covering: The Hidden Assault on our Civil Rights* (New York: Random House, 2006).
14. "Unconscious Bias," LikeForex.com, http://www.likeforex.com/glossary/w/unconscious-bias-3521.

Many individuals in power are not aware that they are making their employment decisions for either hiring or advancement motivated by biases. Yet these entrenched attitudes have repeatedly been revealed by studies showing preferences for white males over minority or female candidates. A 2003 study of race and employer hiring behavior done by Marianne Bertrand and Sendhil Mullainathan is a good example. These researchers altered the names atop two separate résumés while leaving the rest of the résumés identical. Some résumés bore names commonly found on African American birth certificates (such as Lakisha or Jamal), while others bore names commonly found on white birth certificates (such as Emily or Greg). Thus, the same résumé was sometimes presented as that of a presumed African American job seeker and other times, as that of a presumed white job seeker. The researchers found that presumed white applicants were called back approximately 50 percent more often than presumed African American applicants, regardless of industry or occupation.[15] A variant of this type of experiment has been done in the sciences. In one such study, student applications for a laboratory manager position were randomly given a female name or a male name. Not only did faculty participants rate the male applicant as significantly more competent and fit for hire than the female (by factors of 20 percent and 33 percent, respectively), but also the starting recommended salary for men was considerably higher.[16]

Another compelling example of unconscious bias is reflected in the changed audition policies of most of the major U.S. orchestras in the 1970s and the 1980s. Historically, the composition of musicians in the symphony consisted largely of males who may have auditioned along with others but who had then been handpicked by the

---

15. Marianne Bertrand and Sendhil Mullainathan, "Are Emily and Greg More Employable than Lakisha and Jamal? A Field Experiment on Labor Market Discrimination," *The American Economic Review* 94 (Sep 4, 2004): 991–1013.
16. Corinne A. Moss-Racusin, et. al., "Science faculty's subtle gender biases favor male students," *Proceedings of the National Academy of Sciences of the United States of America*, 2012 109 no. 41: 16474–79.

music director of the orchestra. When a decision was made to conduct blind auditions—behind a screen with no visual to influence the decision maker—the diversity of the talent that emerged was different. Among the five highest-ranked orchestras in the nation (located in Boston, Chicago, Cleveland, New York, and Philadelphia), the blind audition process resulted in three times the number of women being hired in little over a decade.[17]

The research studies surrounding unconscious bias and the repeated preferences shown for white males are irrefutable. That being said, it is important to note that every person, whether from a minority group or not, has these biases. This is not to suggest that everyone has a degree of skepticism or even malice in assessing a member of another group. On the contrary, it is merely to demonstrate that all individuals view the world through their own individual lens. Acknowledging that unconscious bias exists and putting in checkpoints, where possible, can help raise awareness and bring more parity.[18]

THE ROLE OF NEW LEGAL MODELS IN INCREASING DIVERSITY AND INCLUSION

There are two unconscious biases that regularly play out in hiring and evaluating legal talent.[19] The first we see is "commitment bias" that often arises with female applicants who are mothers. What lingers underneath the surface is a presumption that mothers are not fully committed to their careers. Instead, there is a concern that their roles as mothers will distract them as employees and result in

---

17.   Claudia Goldin and Cecilia Rouse, "Orchestrating Impartiality: The Impact of 'Blind Auditions on Female Musicians," *The American Economic Review* 90, no. 4 (Sept. 2000): 715–41.

18.   See, e.g., Verna Myers, *Moving Diversity Forward: How to Go from Well-Meaning to Well-Doing* (Chicago: American Bar Association, 2011): 89–92.

19.   Deborah Epstein Henry, *Law & Reorder: Legal Industry Solutions for Restructure, Retention, Promotion & Work/Life Balance* (Chicago: American Bar Association, 2010): 272.

their failure to fully commit to their jobs. The other prevailing bias we see in hiring and evaluating legal talent is "competency bias." Competency bias, as its name suggests, arises from the suspicion that certain individuals are less competent for the job or promotion. In situations where a mother's career path is less linear, for example, some question the lawyer's relevance and whether she can regain the skills and knowledge to be an effective contributor to the profession again. Lawyers in transition often face competency bias as well. For example, when a résumé reflects that a lawyer was part of a large downsizing due to the recession, some may silently question why that individual was the one they chose to let go.

In closely watching the impact of commitment and competency biases,[20] Debbie was excited to discover that secondments may become a compelling way to address unconscious bias in a new light. Training in unconscious bias can be instrumental in raising awareness and reducing the risk of decision making based on unfair assumptions. However, there is arguably no more effective means of remedying unconscious bias risks than allowing individuals to confront those biases directly by engaging and interacting with diverse lawyers. We believe the secondment model presents a powerful opportunity to disrupt the layers of unconscious bias on multiple levels.

When a company decides to bring on a seconded lawyer, it typically uses a different process than it does when making a traditional hire. The company's screening and evaluation process is more removed because the engagement is temporary and because the company's risk is minimized due to the outside secondment firm's assumption of the employment risk. Thus, the alternative hiring approach potentially avoids some of the biases from sneaking into the regular recruiting procedures of many companies.

Once seconded employees get their foot in the door, many companies have found that these lawyers become integral to the

---

20. Ibid.

department. As employers get to know the seconded lawyers who may not have otherwise had the opportunity to demonstrate their ability to contribute and thrive, the one-on-one personal relationship becomes an effective way to address bias. In approximately 15 percent of the cases, Bliss finds that such a "trial period" results in their seconded lawyers converting into permanent employees of their clients' legal departments. If some of these seconded attorneys are women and people of color, secondments can serve as another way for diverse attorneys to enter the marketplace.

When Debbie identified this opportunity to address unconscious bias, she called it "On Deck Diversity" whereby the secondment allows diverse talent already on engagements to fill companies' permanent hiring needs, having already proven themselves ready to deliver. Here is how one of these scenarios played out with a Bliss employee. With strong academics and top law firm and in-house experience, Joanne found herself laid off from a high level in-house investment banking role as a result of the economic downturn of 2008. Joanne pursued an alternative career as a pastry chef and then became a Bliss employee, working for a large financial institution. After proving herself indispensable over the course of 18 months, once a hiring need arose, Joanne became a permanent employee as Chief Legal Officer. With the secondment model at work, Joanne was able to reinvigorate her career without the unconscious biases that may have otherwise thwarted her trajectory to success.

While not every seconded lawyer finds a situation that will, can, or should convert into permanent employment, even in those situations where there is not such an opportunity, we believe the secondment model helps to remedy additional evils that underlie unconscious bias. From the lawyers' perspective, the experience and résumé value of working at in-house legal departments will make these lawyers more marketable for the future, enabling them to become better positioned to find other high level jobs or seek alternative opportunities to enhance their profile. For other diverse lawyers, it may give them the inspiration and confidence to similarly pursue growth opportunities now that they have role models who preceded them. From the company perspective, even if there is not a conversion to permanent employment, clients still gain increased exposure and direct personal experiences working with diverse individuals. We anticipate that this will help to combat their unconscious biases, making them more receptive to a diverse hire in the future.

To be clear, we are not suggesting that secondments are the sole remedy to address unconscious bias for all diverse candidates. Secondments are just one of many employment models, all of which should include a place for diverse lawyers to work and succeed. Instead, we are providing the secondment as one example of how diversity benefits may be gained by changing the employment model. Along these lines, we see temporary positions such as being hired as a summer associate at a law firm or being engaged to perform clinical work as a third-year law student to be other types of On-Deck Diversity opportunities. Like with secondments, these assignments can build a diverse candidate's marketability and create a means to confront unconscious biases through one-on-one interaction. We hope that the secondment and these other examples will provide inspiration for application of On Deck Diversity opportunities in permanent, full-time employment for diverse individuals as well.

OTHER OPPORTUNITIES FOR DIVERSITY AND INCLUSION

Of course, with some firms and companies, diversity is the mission of their work. A minority- or women-owned law firm that is a member of the National Association of Minority & Women Owned Law Firms (NAMWOLF), for example, has woven diversity into its very fabric. In turn, NAMWOLF has become an effective advocate for women and minority-owned law firms to encourage companies to use diversity as a criterion for selection of outside counsel. Additionally, companies certified as female-majority-owned businesses by the Women's Business Enterprise National Council (WBENC) are also likely to make diversity a signature of their work.

The evolving trend we have discussed in prior chapters, where multiple legal service providers team up to represent a client, can also increase opportunities for diverse players as the demands of the client favor collaboration over competition. Clients can aid in this process by tracking large law firms' willingness to partner with and refer business to NAMWOLF firms, WBENC companies and other diverse suppliers.

Taking the true meaning of D&I to heart can create some additional complexities and challenges. An example is when one considers whether diverse law firms should refer business to other diverse legal suppliers and vice versa. The answer seems to be an immediate and resounding yes. So, what if the requirements of membership to NAMWOLF were broader and allowed for all diverse legal suppliers to become members and not just diverse law firms specifically? While this seems like an obvious step, arguably some NAMWOLF firms might face the risk of losing business to other diverse legal suppliers. Even though that risk is present, we would argue that such thinking is too narrow (and we readily admit that this is a self-interested point as Bliss is a WBENC certified business). While it is true that NAMWOLF firms could, at times, be viewed as competitors to other diverse suppliers, they are already facing such competition in banding with other diverse law firms. And, more importantly, if more diverse law firms and diverse legal suppliers worked in concert to provide greater choices for clients, the NAMWOLF membership and collective voice would be even more impactful. The focus should be about increasing the visibility and contribution of all diverse law firms and legal suppliers, thereby enhancing the options for clients. When this concept was put to Joel Stern, the CEO of NAMWOLF, he commented: "Our collective goal is to bring more diversity to the legal profession as a whole with a specific focus on supplier diversity. In an effort to achieve this, we all need to continue to explore creative options that help us enhance diversity and inclusion in the legal profession. Nothing should be left off the table as we have these discussions."[21]

CONCLUSION

D&I that reflects the marketplace will result in a diversity of thought that is far more likely to improve the effective delivery of legal services in the future. Indeed, the research supports that "when teams have one or more members who represent the gender, ethnicity, culture, generation, or sexual orientation of the team's target end user, the entire team is far more likely . . . to understand that target, increasing their likelihood of innovating effectively for that end user."[22] This diversity of thought, represented by the range of backgrounds of different individuals in a room, is what the legal profession needs to more effectively deliver legal services. Those who achieve it will have obtained a competitive advantage and arrived at the intersection of diversity and innovation.

---

21. Based on remarks provided by Joel Stern in a conversation with Deborah Epstein Henry, Philadelphia, PA (April 25, 2014).
22. Sylvia Ann Hewlett, et. al., "Innovation, Diversity, and Market Growth," (Center for Talent Innovation, 2013): 3. (Research found diverse teams were as much as 158 percent more likely to understand their target market.)

7

RELATIONSHIP BUILDING

MICHELE COLEMAN MAYES, VICE PRESIDENT, GENERAL COUNSEL AND SECRETARY, THE NEW YORK PUBLIC LIBRARY; FORMER GENERAL COUNSEL, ALLSTATE INSURANCE COMPANY AND PITNEY BOWES

Developing meaningful relationships can and should be a focus for lawyers at any and every level, whether they are junior associates making their way to their first bar meeting, law firm partners overseeing a successful practice, or general counsel of an internationally known non-profit or for-profit enterprise.

Ours is a profession that thrives on relationships and those attorneys who embrace this are truly the ones who stand out. This does not mean that such attorneys blindly place business cards in every hand or indiscriminately seek to meet anyone with a pulse. Quite the opposite is the case. They are motivated by what interests them first and foremost and they are willing to invest the time to make connections—often unsure of where they might lead.

Continued

MICHELE COLEMAN MAYES, VICE PRESIDENT, GENERAL COUNSEL AND SECRETARY, THE NEW YORK PUBLIC LIBRARY; FORMER GENERAL COUNSEL, ALLSTATE INSURANCE COMPANY AND PITNEY BOWES *CONTINUED*

Anyone who aspires to have an impact in a field that is changing as rapidly, and in as many complex ways as ours, cannot do it alone. Indeed, they know the rewards are far greater when they don't.

While legal practice has evolved over the years, now largely influenced by technology and the likes of social media, the essence remains the same. We are there to help clients, those lawyers earlier in their career and those transitioning to the next phase. This mindset is best captured by the words of a wise person: "What we do for ourselves dies with us. What we do for others and the world is and remains immortal."

INTRODUCTION

We have explored the need to improve the delivery of legal services through various themes including innovation, value, and trust, among others. In addition to addressing those perhaps more obvious concepts, it is important to highlight the need for lawyers to focus on relationship building, particularly as a means to distinguish themselves given the fierce competition in the market. We have come to understand relationship building as investing in a person and that person's interests for the long term, and seeking to help that person as his or her needs and aspirations evolve. Through effective relationship building, lawyers will develop a greater sense of community and stronger networks and, in turn, be able to better meet clients' demands.

The need for lawyers to focus on building meaningful relationships has grown over the past decade. Today, almost half of private practice lawyers in the United States work in solo practice, and another 15 percent work in firms of less than five lawyers.[1] With about two-thirds of lawyers working in practices where they have few, if any, colleagues with whom to confer, the need for effective relationship building and community is heightened. An example where the need for an enhanced lawyer network is evident is in the trend toward disaggregation of work. When work is disaggregated, i.e., separated out, there is a greater need for more collaboration among various legal service providers who combine on a particular representation. Ironically, lawyers from every size firm may feel that billable hour and business development pressures are preventing them from devoting the time to developing close relationships. However, those very pressures contribute to the erosion of connectedness and further the need for community.

THE VALUE OF RELATIONSHIP BUILDING

When in-house lawyers are asked about networking with law firm lawyers, they most often refer to relationship building. What they seek from outside counsel is an interest and investment in the company beyond the matter for which the law firm lawyer is representing the company or a future matter that the law firm lawyer hopes to obtain. As Vice President and Deputy General Counsel of AlliedBarton Security Services, Nancy Peterson shared what she expects from law firm lawyers with whom she works.[2] She wants these lawyers to get to know her company's business beyond the parameters of a specific representation. She wants the lawyer with whom she engages to take the long term view of working with her

---

1. "Lawyer Demographics," American Bar Association, last modified 2012, http://www.americanbar.org/content/dam/aba/migrated/marketresearch/PublicDocuments/lawyer_demographics_2012_revised.authcheckdam.pdf.
2. Based on correspondence with Nancy Peterson and Deborah Epstein Henry, Philadelphia, PA (September 17, 2014).

and investing the time to understand her company's business and its culture.

While in-house lawyers devote much of their attention to their internal clients, they also frequently do outreach to the larger community. In fact, many in-house lawyers say that the hardest transition from law firm to in-house work is the loss of the larger network of law firm colleagues. In response, many in-house lawyers focus on building their outside networks to remain engaged in the community. Karyn Polak, Chief Counsel of the Asset Management Group of PNC Bank relayed that experience when she relocated from another city to join PNC.[3] Despite PNC being a collegial in-house group, Karyn got involved in women's networks and non-profit work not only as a means to give back but also to build her external community and relationships.

While many see the value of developing deep relationships, they are at a loss at how to do so. We find that effective relationship building, in essence, comes down to two things: helping people and engaging in work and activities about which you are passionate. Relationship building is actually a way of being —an approach that you want to be a generous person. As a result of that act of generosity, some people may show a similar generosity towards you, but importantly, we are not talking here about a *quid pro quo*. The difference between an expected barter and providing generous support for others is considerable. *Quid pro quo* is framed as someone doing something in exchange for what can be done in return. Generosity, on the other hand, involves more of a general act of kindness in extending oneself to individuals and making connections for them and otherwise being of assistance. Such support builds positive feelings toward an individual, a good impression that often leads those helped to keep that generosity in mind when an opportunity presents that could be fruitful or of interest.

---

3. Based on remarks provided by Karyn Polak in a conversation with Deborah Epstein Henry, Philadelphia, PA (May 28, 2014).

How do we get to this gesture of goodwill that exists without an expectation of return? Another way of phrasing this question might be: How do we engage in building a relationship that is not conditional? This is where being passionate about your work comes into play. If you are genuine about helping other people make connections, about being a resource and about being accessible, people will inevitably extend themselves to you. Your generosity may not automatically come back to you from every person, or it may come back to you in different venues or wearing a different face than the one you may have expected. Your generosity will, however, infallibly prompt a positive effect in you. But what if you do not find passion in your work or in the venues you seek to network? Claudia Trupp, author and Supervising Attorney of the Center for Appellate Litigation gets this question a lot in the presentations she gives. As someone deeply passionate about her work and her organization's mission, Claudia gives this advice: "Switch jobs! But, in all seriousness, if you can't quit, find passion through pro-bono or volunteer work or other meaningful efforts to fill the void."[4]

One person who has no shortage of passion for her work is Marla Persky, who recently stepped down as Senior Vice President, General Counsel and Secretary of Boehringer Ingelheim USA Corporation. We first met Marla in the summer of 2012 when she and Debbie were the featured speakers at a Connecticut Association of Corporate Counsel event entitled "Empowering Women to Move Forward." Much of the evening's discussion was around inspiring women to network and support each other, subjects near and dear to both Marla's and Debbie's hearts. Since Marla's retirement, she has taken her passion for the subject and made it into her next career, advising law firm clients on how to build an effective network and understand the business of law.

---

4. Based on remarks provided by Claudia Trupp in a conversation with Deborah Epstein Henry, New York, NY (April 22, 2014).

The bottom line about relationship building can be captured in this quote often attributed to Winston Churchill: "You make a living by what you get; you make a life by what you give."[5] This quote conveys the spirit of generosity that we espouse. It also demonstrates that while we are talking about the value of relationship building in your career, this concept is broader as it pertains to your life. This more expansive view of relationship building is what clients want and what will allow you to service their needs better as you get to know them both as colleagues and as people.

DEVELOPING STRATEGIC ALLIANCES

There are some strategic considerations to keep in mind as one invests in building relationships. Being selective about where attorneys put their efforts makes sense in a profession where time is limited and many practitioners already feel overextended. What you do not want to do, however, is to make the mistake of only designating certain people as "important." Many people falsely predetermine those who are worthy of their time. This can leave a legitimately bad taste in the mouths of those who did not make the grade. In fact, individuals who believe they can determine who is worthy and who is not worthy are often very transparent, and those who get cut from their list will likely never forget it.

Being selective can work the other way as well. When we talk about relationship building, we are not simply talking about pressing a card into everyone's hand at a networking event. This is where the second guideline of relationship building comes in: focusing on areas of passion. If you are focused on issues that you care about, where you can actually contribute and where you want to be playing an integral role, then you will naturally be more judicious about your time and develop strategic alliances that are genuine.

---

5.   Liz Weiss, "10 Famous Quotes that are Misattributed," *Business Insider*, last modified July 27, 2011, http://www.businessinsider.com/10-famous-quotes -that-are-misattributed-2011-7?op=1.

The value of generous and passionate relationship building is manifold. The legal profession thrives on the synergy of mutual beneficiaries. These may be easier to engage in when relationships are more obviously noncompetitive, such as when two law firms from different geographies or substantive expertise pair on a representation. Such introductions can lead to valuable reciprocal referrals, but the depth and effectiveness of relationship building does not truly expand until we begin to know people outside of these initial confines. When we build relationships effectively, we get to know the whole person with whom we are relating, and can then be that much greater a resource.

Effective relationship building for law firm lawyers also means keeping in regular touch and getting to know the office culture of the company you are seeking to represent, not just attempting to swoop in when a potential matter arises. Robin Smith, General Counsel and Corporate Secretary at LEGO Systems, Inc. captured this point in a panel discussion where she talked about the do's and don'ts of networking.[6] Robin recounted an outside lawyer visiting the LEGO offices and being unable to comprehend the office culture that allows the LEGO employees to ride down the hallways on scooters and test and experience the various LEGO products. She knew immediately this visitor was not someone who could ever represent her company because he could not appreciate who they were and what they deliver. Any lawyer she would hire would need to be able to engage and understand the fun in the LEGO product in order to provide the best counsel. And while lawyers may not necessarily have to be users of clients' products, at a minimum they must understand their clients' businesses and their concerns as well as the spirit of their companies.

---

6. Based on remarks provided by Robin Smith as a panelist at a conference, Wilmington, DE (March 25, 2011).

THE ROLES OF TECHNOLOGY AND SOCIAL MEDIA IN RELATIONSHIP BUILDING

While many lawyers are uncertain about how to effectively build relationships, we see that uncertainty often heightens into anxiety in the context of social media. This anxiety, at times, presents itself as cynicism that social media cannot be used as a replacement for in-person communication. We agree—we are not advocating that one mode of communication replace the other. What we maintain is that social media can be another tool to build relationships, and that proper use of social media can have an efficient and powerful impact. Additionally, this connectivity can help strengthen community by bringing together different people with whom you have relationships.

When we consider the effect of social media in building relationships, the old marketing adage—The Rule of Seven—comes to mind. The Rule of Seven says that a prospective customer needs to see or hear your marketing message at least seven times before he or she will take action to hire or buy from you.[7] Every lawyer, law firm, company, and legal service provider has a brand that needs to be built and maintained. Those seven impressions that the advertising world says it takes to register your brand with a consumer (in this case, the client) can be greatly enhanced through social media. As a legal professional this is no different, and social media is a means to allow those impressions to continue to be reinforced. Every time someone hears you express an opinion, share a timely or noteworthy link, or give a talk, social media enhances your presence and visibility.

Technology allows for an efficient use of time, enabling you to reach many more people through a keystroke than you could through daily contact or attending a cocktail reception. We have

---

7. Andrea Stenberg, "What is the Rule of Seven? And How Will it Improve Your Marketing?" The Baby Boomer Entrepreneur, last modified October 17, 2008, http://the babyboomerentrepreneur.com/258/what-is-the-rule-of-seven-and-how-will-it-i mprove-your-marketing/.

seen lawyers used LinkedIn, for example, to help others identify business opportunities, learn new ideas, and raise their profile to help ensure job security. Some of these lawyers are deliberate in building their networks early in their careers and embracing a routine where they add new connections at the end of each day or week. Social media may not be the entire future, but it is a large part of what is yet to come—it can and should be harnessed to enhance the extent of your visibility, the capacity of your reach, and the impact of your message.

RELEVANCY AND THE ROLE OF THE BAR IN RELATIONSHIP BUILDING

Much of the discussion around relationship building focuses on establishing strong one-on-one relationships. However, a significant value to building more meaningful relationships is the cumulative effect of establishing stronger communities. The difficulties we identified in attaining community are particularly acute for the nearly two-thirds of all lawyers working in solo practices or small firms. Compounding the isolation is that many of these solo and small firm practitioners are located in geographically dispersed areas. Given that most attorneys desire to be connected, not to mention mentored, these needs have traditionally been fulfilled by bar associations whether on the national, state, or local level.

As a consultant to the New York State Bar Association in 2008, Debbie participated in the Special Committee on Balanced Lives in the Law that released a report examining changes to the legal profession that led to work/life dissatisfaction among attorneys.[8] One of the key challenges cited involved lawyers becoming increasingly overworked so that their time was more constrained: They had

---

8.   Catherine M. Richardson, et al., "Final Report," New York State Bar Association, last modified March 7, 2008, http://www.nysba.org/WorkArea/DownloadAsset .aspx?id=26859.

less time for pro-bono work and fewer opportunities to become involved with their bar associations. Since the economic downturn, the challenge with respect to bar association engagement has become more pronounced. During the recession, attorneys felt the need to focus that much more on their business, and they questioned whether the time devoted to the bar was going to generate the return they needed and provide the forum for relationship building that they sought. In addition, it was harder for some firms—which traditionally footed the cost of membership in the bar for their lawyers—to justify the expense of membership dues when they were looking for as many ways as possible to reduce costs. Exacerbating these concerns, many bar associations have been slow to adapt to the changing face of technology, making practitioners further question how a bar association will raise their visibility and profile.

The ambivalence towards the bar is more of a recent phenomenon. Membership in bar associations was how many lawyers in the baby boomer generation built their practice, developed their reputation, and grew their networks. Generation Y attorneys, however, have different expectations of the kinds of resources they will need to build relationships and how those resources will be accessed and delivered. Since the demands of attorneys have changed, bar associations will need to pay attention to the full range of demographics they serve in order to remain relevant.

By our accounts, bar associations can still provide a crucial connection for junior lawyers, assuming they can find the right means of communication to reach them. Bar associations can also be instrumental in providing Gen Y attorneys with leadership opportunities that may not come as readily elsewhere in the earlier stages of their careers. These volunteer roles can greatly increase a junior lawyer's exposure, and it will be up to the bar associations to demonstrate that deliverable through technology savvy and know how.

OTHER WAYS TO MAKE THE BAR MORE RELEVANT TO HELPING LAWYERS BUILD RELATIONSHIPS

In Chapter 5, where we focus on Talent Development, we proposed an organizational push to outsource the training function of junior lawyers. Educating junior lawyers in the core competencies required for the legal profession would be a significant opportunity for bar associations to become more integral to the legal community. Bar associations could also serve as a training platform for senior lawyers who are approaching retirement and have the interest and skill to become adjunct teachers. Such an effort would thereby preserve the baby boomers' accumulated wisdom and knowledge by transferring it to the younger generation while simultaneously fulfilling much of the training and mentoring needs that Gen Y lawyers seek. Having bar associations become partners in training lawyers could increase practical skills and mentorship, streamline transitions, provide a meaningful forum for lawyers to build relationships, and reduce cost—all by serving the profession in a very meaningful way.

Bar associations could also serve to foster another aspect of relationship building—providing sponsorship opportunities for junior lawyers and the community at large. Sponsorship is an increasingly familiar concept whereby powerful people are willing to put their trust and support behind a high-potential individual to further his or her advancement. One compelling sponsorship example is how a prominent in-house lawyer at an investment bank sponsored an underprivileged New York high school student who ultimately became the valedictorian of his high school, earning him a scholarship to MIT. This attorney, who is passionate about helping people progress professionally, also (on a less formal basis) serves as a mentor for in-house and outside counsel and has been instrumental in supporting these attorneys with professional development. Bar associations could provide the venue and breeding ground for these relationships to flourish and then provide similar life-changing opportunities for attorneys.

Bar associations should also consider assuming other roles to provide needed education to attorneys and, in turn, create another place for not only learning but also relationship building. They can take the lead in the technological curve, helping train junior lawyers in social media for the purposes of networking and teaching solo practitioner and small firm lawyers how to gain an effective online presence. They can also offer entrepreneurship education. Newly minted lawyers have for the most part not been taught how to manage their legal practice as a business. Bar associations should also be more willing to broaden their programming to explore the use of a law degree for roles outside of practice.

CONCLUSION

There are many positive aspects of relationship building—helping others, identifying business opportunities, facilitating connections, raising profiles, advancing meaningful causes, making friends, and having fun. By being more deliberate and focused on what attorneys can bring to the people with whom they have relationships and those with whom they would like to have relationships, attorneys can bring more satisfaction and purpose to the lives of others as well as their own.

By going beyond one-on-one relationships, attorneys can bring the depth of their connections to the broader legal community. For bar associations to be effective in helping lawyers build relationships, it will mean changing their means of communication, programming, approach, and positioning to empower lawyers to pursue practice with the backing and platform that they need. With these collaborative efforts, we will ideally bring back the value of community and help build relationships to enable lawyers and legal service providers to better navigate the challenges in the marketplace of today and tomorrow.

CONCLUSION: HAPPY CLIENTS, HAPPY LAWYERS

GRETCHEN RUBIN, AUTHOR, *THE HAPPINESS PROJECT* AND *HAPPIER AT HOME*; FORMER LAW CLERK, JUSTICE SANDRA DAY O'CONNOR

The title of this chapter is "Happy Clients, Happy Lawyers." Some people may argue that in today's environment of economic uncertainty and widespread cut-backs, happiness is a luxury that clients and lawyers can ill afford.

But in fact, research shows—and everyday experience confirms—that happiness isn't a frivolous luxury at work. In one of those life-isn't-fair results, it turns out that the happy outperform the less happy.

Happy people are more altruistic, more productive, and more helpful. They're more creative in solving problems—and more resilient when things go wrong. Because people prefer to be around happier people, happy people work better with others, and they make better team members, as well as better leaders. They're healthier, and they have healthier habits. Happy people

Continued

> **GRETCHEN RUBIN, AUTHOR, *THE HAPPINESS PROJECT* AND *HAPPIER AT HOME*; FORMER LAW CLERK, JUSTICE SANDRA DAY O'CONNOR *CONTINUED***
>
> are less likely to show counterproductive work behaviors like burn-out, absenteeism, disputes, or counter- and non-productive work, than are less-happy people.
>
> When we're unhappy, we tend to become defensive, isolated, and preoccupied with our own problems. It's hard for us to turn outward, to think about the problems of other people or the challenges at work.
>
> Time, energy, and money spent to foster the happiness of clients and lawyers are resources well spent—both for the individuals affected and the firms and companies that employ them.

INTRODUCTION

Is it possible—as our subtitle indicates—to have both happy clients and happy lawyers in the volatile legal market of today and tomorrow? In this book, we have tried to convey how to create happy clients and happy lawyers by improving the understanding and delivery of legal services in seven key areas. The future for success in the profession lies in improving the alignment between clients and lawyers. Happy clients are ones who have created a hospitable workplace such that their employees are more productive. These happy clients have also fostered a mutually beneficial relationship with their outside legal service providers. As a result, their business is more profitable. Happy lawyers are ones who feel valued and enjoy both the substance of their work and the lifestyle it affords them; they are, in turn, more satisfied, productive, dedicated and loyal employees.

In between happy clients and happy lawyers are happy legal service providers, including happy law firms. Much of this book has addressed the need for law firms to evolve, so it would be remiss not to mention: happy legal service providers, including happy law firms, are what connect happy clients and happy lawyers. Law firms and other legal service providers that are able to facilitate this connection are not only the ones who will enhance the quality of life—the "happiness" factor of all involved—but also they are the ones who will survive in the long run.

INNOVATION
Happy Clients
In terms of Innovation, happy clients are first and foremost those who are presented with greater variety in their choice of who and how they will be represented. Legal service providers need to be experts in the services they deliver to clients, allowing them to provide those services at a more competitive price and with greater efficiency while performing at a higher level. That is what clients really want, and it will take ingenuity to deliver. Given the increased pressure in the marketplace, clients are looking for that creativity now more than ever.

Accompanying creativity, clients want clarity about which legal service provider should perform each disaggregated piece of work and guidance about how to ensure a coordinated execution of the work. Project management is an important skill that happy clients seek, given the increasing number of alternative resources that exist in the profession today. Whether this project management is internally or externally directed, happy clients are looking for delegation, communication and accountability to help ensure their trust and satisfaction.

Happy Lawyers
Happy Lawyers seek to apply the advantages of innovation to both where and how they practice. They want more choice in the

range of venues in which they use their law degree, in the type of substantive work in which they are engaged, and also in how that work affects their lifestyle. With more choice, more lawyers may elect to remain in the legal field in a non-practicing capacity—these are lawyers who otherwise may have left the field altogether.

All lawyers will benefit from an increased focus in the profession on innovation and creativity. Skill sets that have not been fully tapped, given the historic risk aversive nature cultivated in lawyers, can now be used to deconstruct some of the traditional notions of a lawyer's role. Systems which tend toward facilitating the business rather than obstructing it are what will inspire lawyers of the future to be more responsive to clients' needs. Happy lawyers will be the ones who are rewarded for helping companies make things happen, at a higher skill level and in a more cost efficient way.

VALUE
Happy Clients

With regard to value, what makes clients happy are meaningful alternative fee arrangements that align their interests with those of the legal service providers that represent them. Clients do not want to have to wait until they ask for these arrangements either. They want the law firm lawyers with whom they work to initiate conversations about creative alternative fee structures and they want their law firms to have an infrastructure in place to implement these alternatives seamlessly and immediately. Simple, creative alternatives that are workable and fair, with appropriate checkpoints so no one feels taken advantage of, are what clients are seeking in how their matters are billed.

While the billable hour may remain for certain representations, for clients it will be far more valuable over the long run to evaluate a lawyer's contributions based on the Value Measure of Quality of Work, Efficiency, and Results Achieved. To reach this goal, happy clients desire a meaningful link between the work done and the lawyer doing it—clients want the work demands to accurately mirror the experience and skill level of the lawyer who is performing the work.

Happy Lawyers

Happy lawyers want the profession to embrace a range of viable and valued career paths. What this means is creating different models for success where career engagement, promotion opportunities, and job satisfaction are the motivations for individual choices, rather than simply avoiding one option where a stigma may be attached.

Happy lawyers also want an acknowledgement in the profession that life often intervenes and in some cases necessitates the need or desire for a non-linear career path. They want a viable means to switch paths or leave the profession and to be able to redirect or return again. They want to be welcomed back for the contribution that they can continue to make, assuming that the needs of the business can support their redirection or return.

Finally, happy lawyers want to be valued on a measure other than time. They want to be evaluated for their quality of their work, efficiency and results achieved rather than hours logged.

PREDICTABILITY AND TRUST
Happy Clients

Happy clients want predictability in their fees—they do not want any surprises when it comes to their budgets. To achieve this predictability, clients need effective communication—and not only about fees but about what the full scope of a representation entails as well as the viable case strategies. No one expects their lawyers to have a crystal ball, but being able to anticipate and communicate to clients what the various outcomes may be and whether mid-course changes are necessary enhances proper planning and the ability for fully-informed clients to position themselves strategically.

Predictability thus encourages trust in the lawyer/client relationship, which is what really makes clients happy. Clients seek the sincere belief that they are getting the best service for the best value, and that they have hired the best legal service provider to represent them based on both the counsel and the service they receive.

Happy Lawyers

For happy lawyers, predictability stems from the feeling that the daily pace and structure of their life is under control. While the nature of legal work is such that, at times, this is not possible, when it is an achievable goal, it is one that employers should support. By gaining more predictability in their place of employment, and performing high level, engaging work, lawyers will be more productive and find more satisfaction in their life inside and outside of work.

Just as predictability leads to trust for the happy client, so the lawyer who is able to gain predictability in his or her work and in turn feel the trust in his or her colleagues expand. A happy lawyer is one who works in an environment where colleagues are predictable in their approach and fair in their treatment of each other. This means that credit will be given when appropriate and allocated where it is due. Getting recognition for being part of meaningful work or generating a client relationship is more important than simply earning money or putting oneself in line for a promotion; these aspects may be practically important but they do not result in happiness. A truly happy lawyer is one who is part of a team pursuing something greater than any individual accomplishment.

FLEXIBILITY
Happy Clients

Happy clients want the ability to expand and contract staff in order to mirror their actual workflow. Given their uncertainty in staffing needs, clients want to be able to bring on experts when the work demands it, but not to have to carry extra payroll when that workload shifts. Thus, clients are happy to avoid absorbing employment risks and increasing headcount. Additionally, in a world where there is no longer a 9 to 5 clock—instead, work is being done at all times—happy clients want the lawyers with whom they work to be flexible, responsive and accessible when pressing work needs arise.

Additionally, happy clients are ones who are part of the decision-making process and strategic thinking in a representation. They do not want to be presented with a *fait accompli* that does not provide an opportunity for incorporating their feedback. They want to feel like they are making a meaningful contribution and partnering with advisors who are flexible and work in concert to determine the best solution.

Flexibility also includes openness on the part of a client's lawyers to changing course when new information dictates there may be a better choice or direction. Flexibility is thus an expansiveness of mind, an elasticity born of humility and a true partnership.

Happy Lawyers

Happy lawyers want the flexibility to work differently. This is not about accommodation on the part of an employer, but rather maximizing the productivity of individuals who approach their work with integrity. Happy lawyers can apply flexibility to the location where they work, the time frames in which they work, and the methods they use to communicate with those whom they work—all the while ensuring that their quality of work, responsiveness and accessibility are not negatively impacted. Happy lawyers who have more control in the way in which they work are far more likely to provide reciprocity, and in turn greater value, to their employers in terms of flexibility by working nights and weekends, when necessary, to create a win-win situation.

TALENT DEVELOPMENT
Happy Clients
Clients who do not have to absorb the cost and responsibility of training junior lawyers are happy clients. They do not want to be billed for having inexperienced yet expensive lawyers staffed on their matters. They want to know who is working on their matters and they do not want to see new names on their bills without an explanation. They want to understand the talent pool that is being assigned to their work and know that the decisions made behind who is being staffed are fair to them as well as being fair to the firm that made them. In other words, happy clients want a thoughtfulness to be brought to how they are represented. More specifically, this means matching a lawyer with the appropriate level of experience and seniority to what the work demands, keeping in mind both efficiency and cost effectiveness as well as the results and the quality of work.

Happy Lawyers
Happy lawyers want jobs—that is, they want to be practicing lawyers in the first place. They want to graduate law school without an overwhelming amount of debt and enter a profession that does not shirk its responsibility for developing and training new talent. Happy lawyers want the confidence and security that their commitment to the profession will be returned when they enter the legal market. They want and need professional development opportunities not only when they are starting their career but also as that career continues to take shape.

But junior lawyers are not the only ones transitioning in the legal profession who need help; baby boomers approaching retirement likewise want professional development opportunities. Happy baby boomer lawyers are ones who are valued and rewarded for their institutional knowledge as well as the depth of their relationships and their practical know-how. These lawyers will be happy if given a platform to educate younger lawyers about how to become a trusted advisor and how to run a business. In this case, happiness is having one's wealth of experience honored and passed down to the next generation of talent.

DIVERSITY AND INCLUSION
Happy Clients

Happy clients are those who have more diverse choices in the types of lawyers who represent them and in the types of legal service providers with whom they partner. By working with diverse lawyers from different backgrounds, happy clients see that the deliverable at the end of the day is inevitably better. Happy clients value inclusive work environments that allow people to be more authentic which in turn enables them to be more productive and greater contributors.

Happy Lawyers

Happy lawyers are those who are able to overcome unconscious bias and gain access to legitimate opportunities. By getting a fair foot in the door, happy lawyers are able to demonstrate their value and what they can do for the team. Happy are the lawyers who find inclusive work environments where they feel they can be themselves. They experience consistency in their identity at work and outside of the office, which in turn affects their loyalty, as well as the results they can deliver to their employer.

RELATIONSHIP BUILDING
Happy Clients

When lawyers maintain regular communications out of a genuine interest in having an engaged, ongoing relationship—that makes for happy clients. Clients do not want to feel used or called upon only when a lawyer hears that a new representation is arising and there might be work on the table.

Happy clients want their legal service providers to get to know them personally and they want them to get to know the nature of their business and the culture of their company. They also want to feel part of a group beyond their in-house department, where they can draw from the knowledge of a larger network of colleagues and contribute to the community at large.

Happy Lawyers

Happy lawyers are those who find the generosity and passion that leads to successful relationship building. Such lawyers enjoy the opportunity both to help others and to engage in outside activities where they feel like they can make a significant contribution. Meaningful one-on-one relationship building leads to a more enriched legal community, giving happy lawyers a network, a support base and an informational resource which is particularly necessary in today's volatile and isolating market.

CONCLUSION

When we set out in search of bliss, the notion of identifying what constitutes happy clients and happy lawyers felt like a wish list of sorts. Over time it has become more than a wish list—it has become our reality. It may sound idyllic, but that is why we wrote this book. In our own lives, we have demonstrated that it is possible to have both happy clients and happy lawyers. Our hope is that this book will inspire you to similarly take your wishes and achieve happiness. In turn, you will gain the productivity, profitability and satisfaction in your work and life —otherwise known as bliss.

INDEX